Copyright January 9, 2016
Published February 9, 2016
All rights reserved to Barbara Ball

This book is dedicated to the community of adult children caring for their aging parents and offers education and resources before the crisis happens.

"We never touch someone so lightly that we don't leave a piece of ourselves behind. Be kind."

Book reviews:

"Well written with compassion, amazing and informative. A must for anyone needing direction & advice in healthcare."

Sonia H, Healthcare Rep, Phoenix, AZ

"This is an excellent book that helped me understand the terms and language used by doctors and nurses and offers such amazing resources for further assistance. It's an amazing book!"

M. Sue Wilkins, Caregiver, Tulsa, OK

"My company asked Barbara for something like this and she came through. After reading it from cover to cover I found it so helpful and it gave me such clarity, and I work in healthcare. It's a must read for everyone!"

Liz Rodriguez, STI Rehab, Phoenix, AZ

Luke 10:30-37

Jesus replied,

"A man was going down from Jerusalem to Jericho, and he fell among robbers, who stripped him and beat him and departed, leaving him half dead. Now by chance a priest was going down that road, and when he saw him he passed by on the other side. So, likewise a Levite, when he came to the place and saw him, passed by on the other side. But a Samaritan, as he journeyed, came to where he was, and when he saw him, he had compassion.

He went to him and bound up his wounds, pouring on oil and wine. Then he set him on his own animal and brought him to an inn and took care of him.

For my brother, Robert Earl Ball, who inspired me to write this book and taught me what forgiveness and true love really mean.

                Date Of Birth -   February 9, 1954
                Date Of Death - February 9, 2016

"Sail away with fair winds and calm seas, to the Heavens and beyond, my Sailor brother!"

TABLE OF CONTENTS

Chapter 1	Introduction	Page 9
Chapter 2	Types of Services	Page 11
Chapter 3	Long Term Stay	Page 17
Chapter 4	A New Home	Page 26
Chapter 5	Hospice Explained	Page 31
Chapter 6	Veteran's Benefits	Page 43
Chapter 7	Other Legal Services	Page 45
Chapter 8	The Importance of Life Insurance	Page 49
Chapter 9	Burial & Funeral Services	Page 50
Chapter 10	Medicaid vs. Medicare	Page 52
Chapter 11	Family Gathering & The Talk	Page 56
Chapter 12	The Stages of Grief	Page 59
Chapter 13	Understanding the Clinical Side	Page 68
Chapter 14	Caregiver Stress	Page 69
Chapter 15	Dementia – Sundowners & Alzheimer's	Page 71
Chapter 16	Death & the Physical Body	Page 82
Chapter 17	The Dying Process	Page 87
Chapter 18	End of Life Nutrition	Page 91
Chapter 19	Terminal Agitation	Page 94
Chapter 20	Resource Links	Page 97

Chapter 1
INTRODUCTION

First and foremost, let me explain that I am not certified as a clinician, I am just like you. I am an everyday person who has worked in the field of hospice and home health for many years and discovered the biggest gap is within the community pertaining to education of the healthcare system, resources and what decisions to make when your loved one or aging parent needs you to step in and help them in their time of need and crisis.

For many years I have worked in the field of hospice as a liaison and educator of physicians, clinicians and local communities to inform on the many different resources available to families and patients. I advocate for the family, the adult children and the person suffering from the diagnosis of their terminal illness.

Knowledge is empowerment and the key to peace is knowing you have provided the services needed for your aging or other loved ones.
The one thing we all have in common other than our family genetics, is that we are all born, and we will all die. For me, it's not a question of what makes a great life such as wealth, money, material items and the like, but rather what makes for a good and quality end of life. Because once we are born and reach a certain age, our bodies begin the slow process of decline to the inevitable conclusion of death. Is death such a bad thing, I believe not. I've personally witnessed many deaths during the actual active dying stage, and the privilege of being present in the moment of those who are passing from this journey on to the next is what I term, spectacular and amazing. I was with my father for the last four and half months of his life and present when he was actively dying, and I can tell you that he truly died a good and peaceful death. The blessings he bestowed on me during his last months of life in this realm were a mere glimpse into the next realm and journey. His example offered me comfort in knowing there is so much awaiting us beyond the veil of this Earthly realm.

I've been around the elderly most of my life starting with my mother who was a nurse at a nursing home in Oregon. Then the loss of my brother Tony at my tender age of 15 was devastating, to say the least. He was killed by a drunk driver while home on leave from the Military for the holidays. Years later, my father became my first hospice experience and passed from COPD. I was also diagnosed with cancer in 2007 and feel that I am remaining here with the purpose to educate and serve others.

Ironically, working in the healthcare field the past several years and being involved with death and dying has offered great insight regarding the dynamic of those involved. From siblings to parents, to extended family members demonstrating what I've noticed most, is that the person with the diagnosis typically knows and accepts their limited time but it is the family that remains in denial. Ellen Kubler-Ross wrote about the Stages of Grief outlining the emotional factors for those who are faced with the impending death of a loved one. What we fail to understand is that this process applies to the family and loved ones before the person actually passes away too. In my own experience, I've noticed that we vacillate from one emotion to the next frequently when we have a loved one who is faced with a debilitating illness that will ultimately lead to their death and this is perfectly natural and okay. The issue is when we fail to recognize or deny that this is the time to bond, make new memories, fulfill bucket lists and enjoy and share all the love we have with our terminally ill loved one. It doesn't matter what happened in the past or present, what matters is what we do now from this point on. Specifically, the whole process and journey of life is about unconditional love and acceptance, even of death.

So, my intent and purpose here is to break it down and assist in offering resources and education to all, so that when the time comes you are not frantic and drowning in chaos. You can help and enjoy your loved one as it was meant to be.

Chapter 2
TYPES OF SERVICES

First, let's discuss the different types of services that you will become familiar with regarding the condition of your loved one.

Home Health
This is a rehabilitative service meant to get the person back to their original state of physical functioning or close to it. It is what I refer to as the "happy" medical services and while it may be painful for the patient, it usually assists them in returning to a better physical state.

Home Health services are paid for by insurance or the Medicare benefit for up to 100 days and then the patient is discharged or D/C'd as it is referred to in medical terms. Medicare (CMS) has very rigid guidelines and policies which require extensive documentation in order for the patient to maintain these services. Be aware that as the time draws closer to the final payment, the patient will not be able to continue these unless documentation can be provided showing the need to continue. Even then, Medicare or your private insurance company can decline payment.

Be careful that you aren't placed in a position of not understanding this and getting an astronomical bill because you didn't know that the payer source ceased payment.

In discussing home health, I feel it necessary to inform you that an 80 year old person will not benefit from rehabilitative services and typically just want to be left alone. Sometimes they are subjected to surgeries for their hip and the like, just as a means for the surgeon and hospital to make more money. It won't help your grandma or grandpa reach a quality of life and can sometimes even advance their decline. Just be cognizant that this is an elderly person who wants a "quality of life", not to get up and do the swing to the big band song they once loved.

Physical & Occupational Therapy

Both therapies are for improving the patient's abilities to return to similar or normal way of life. These are highly regulated services and are typically paid for by private insurance and/or Medicare/Medicaid.

You cannot have these services if you are on hospice as they are considered "curative" services with the intent to return the person back to as normal a state of being as before the injury or incident.

Occupational Therapy

As compared with Physical Therapy, occupational therapy tends to focus more on evaluating and improving a person's functional abilities. An occupational therapist often does not directly treat a person's injury using techniques such as manual therapy or acupuncture like a physical therapist would but more commonly helps a person optimize their independence and their ability to accomplish their daily activities following an injury or in situations of physical impairment.

Occupational therapists often will directly treat injuries, but more even often occupational therapy focuses more on improving life skills and incorporating adaptive tools at times customized by the therapist. In some parts of the world occupational therapists utilize practices such as use of ultrasound in injury rehabilitation, much like a physical therapist does.

Helping people improve their ability to carry out their daily tasks is a prime goal of the occupational therapist. An OT is more likely to perform on-site assessments of both the home environment and work environment and give recommendations on suitable adaptations of each to allow for a better quality of life. The occupational therapist is trained to modifying the physical environment as well as training the person to use assistive equipment to increase independence. While physical therapists do on-site assessments as well this tends to be less common.

Physical Therapy / Physiotherapy

The physical therapy profession (also called 'physiotherapy' in many parts of the world) tends to be more focused on evaluating and diagnosing movement dysfunctions as well as treating a person's injury itself. While an occupational therapist will often also do diagnosis, the physical therapist will be more likely to diagnose and treat the physical source of the problem; the injured tissues and structures.

Both physical and occupational therapists are trained extensively in anatomy and the musculoskeletal system resulting in both being very knowledgeable about musculoskeletal injuries and rehabilitation than a general practitioner medical doctor.

Overlap Between OT and PT

Although the two health care professions have differences in their focus there is much crossover between OT and PT. For an example of the crossover, an occupational therapist is often involved in educating people on how to prevent and avoid injuries, as well as educating people about the healing process, just like a physical therapist. Physical therapists in turn often help people improve their ability to do their daily activities through education and training. While there is this crossover between professions both play very important roles and are specialized in their areas of expertise. In many situations, both types of health-care professional are involved in injury recovery.

http://physicaltherapyweb.com/differences-occupational-therapy-physical-therapy/

Medicare Limits on Therapy Services

** Important: This information only applies if you have Original Medicare. If you have a Medicare Advantage Plan (like an HMO or PPO), check with your plan for information about your plan's coverage rules on therapy services.

Medicare law limits how much it pays for your medically necessary outpatient therapy services in one calendar year. These limits are called "therapy caps" or "therapy cap limits."

What are the outpatient therapy cap limits for 2016?

- $1,960 for physical therapy (PT) and speech-language pathology (SLP) services combined
- $1,960 for occupational therapy (OT) services

After you pay your yearly deductible for Medicare Part B (Medical Insurance), Medicare pays its share (80%), and you pay your share (20%) of the cost for the therapy services. The Part B deductible is $166 for 2016. Medicare will pay its share for therapy services until the total amount paid by both you and Medicare reaches either one of the therapy cap limits. Amounts paid by you may include costs like the deductible and coinsurance.

Can I get an exception to the therapy cap limits?

You may qualify for an exception to the therapy cap limits (which would allow Medicare to pay for services after you reach the therapy cap limits) if you get medically necessary PT, SLP, and/or OT services over the $1,960 therapy cap limit. See the next page for more information.

Who can give me outpatient therapy services?
You can get outpatient therapy from any of these health care professionals:
- Physical therapists
- Speech-language pathologists
- Occupational therapists

Doctors and other health care professionals (like nurse practitioners, clinical nurse specialists, and physician assistants) may also offer PT, SLP, and OT services. Revised January 2016.

Where can I get outpatient therapy services?
- Offices of privately practicing therapists
- Many medical offices
- Outpatient hospital departments, including those of critical access hospitals (CAHs)
- Rehabilitation agencies (sometimes called "other rehabilitation facilities" (ORFs))
- Comprehensive outpatient rehabilitation facilities (CORFs)
- Skilled nursing facilities (SNFs) when Part A doesn't apply
- At home, from certain therapy providers, like privately practicing therapists and certain home health agencies (if you aren't under a home health plan of care)

What can I do if I need medically necessary services that will go above the outpatient therapy cap limits?
You may qualify to get an exception to the therapy cap limits so that Medicare will continue to pay its share for your therapy services after you reach the therapy cap limits. Your therapist or therapy provider must:
- Establish your need for medically reasonable and necessary services and document this in your medical record
- Indicate on your Medicare claim for services above the therapy cap limit that your therapy services are medically reasonable and necessary

As part of the exceptions process, there are additional limits (called "thresholds"). If you get outpatient therapy services higher than the threshold amounts, a Medicare contractor may review your medical records to check for medical necessity. The threshold amounts for 2016 are:

- $3,700 for PT and SLP combined
- $3,700 for OT

In general (when an exceptions process is in effect), if your therapist or therapy provider provides documentation to show that your services were medically reasonable and necessary and indicates this on your claim, Medicare will continue to cover its share above the $1,960 therapy cap limits.

** Hospice – See Chapter 5

Chapter 3

LONG TERM STAY

Hospital stay

Medicare and private insurance typically pay for hospital stays with a flat rate amount and length of stay (days) determination. The DRG (diagnosis related group) is set forth by CMS and this is how the determination is applied for the length of stay at the hospital. A hospital will get a set amount for the length of stay. For instance, you are admitted for a surgery which is paid for at 6 days stay in the hospital. The hospital will reduce your length of stay and this is why people are always shocked when they get a call from the discharge planner stating they are sending you home tomorrow and you thought you had two more days to recover.

Be aware there was a new regulation put out by the federal government limiting payment for "Frequent Flyers" who are repeatedly going to the hospital or emergency room. A hospital cannot admit a patient for the same diagnosis within a 30 day timeframe and get paid for it. To get around this they often put the patient in the hospital overnight under the "Observation" status. If you go in with chest pain and are sent home, then return again before 30 days is up for chest pain again, the odds are the hospital will not get paid for this event. And it doesn't matter if you go to a different hospital or emergency room, it will still be monitored.

https://www.cms.gov/medicare/medicare-fee-for-service-payment/acuteinpatientpps/readmissions-reduction-program.html

https://www.law.cornell.edu/cfr/text/42/412.154

Hospital Ranking by State

http://www.hospitalsafetyscore.org/your-hospitals-safety-score/state-rankings

https://www.medicare.gov/hospitalcompare/search.html

Does your state make the grade? Hospitals across the country show great variation when it comes to patient safety. Here states are ranked based on the percentage of "A" hospitals they have compared to the total number of hospitals that operate in that state. Maryland is not ranked because hospitals are not required to publicly report their hospital safety data.

Rank	State	Number of A Hospitals	Number of Graded Hospitals	Percent (%) of A Hospitals
1	Maine	11	16	68.8%
2	Massachusetts	35	58	60.3%
3	Florida	92	163	56.4%
4	Virginia	34	64	53.1%
5	New Jersey	32	67	47.8%
6	Illinois	51	117	43.6%
7	Tennessee	27	67	40.3%
8	North Carolina	30	79	38.0%
9	Colorado	15	40	37.5%
10	Georgia	24	69	34.8%
11	California	88	254	34.6%
12	South Dakota	2	6	33.3%
13	Texas	67	203	33.0%
14	Utah	7	22	31.8%
15	Ohio	30	107	28.0%
16	Idaho	3	11	27.3%
17	Arizona	12	45	26.7%
18	Wisconsin	12	46	26.1%
19	Kentucky	12	49	24.5%
20	Louisiana	11	46	23.9%
21	Michigan	19	80	23.8%
22	Pennsylvania	31	131	23.7%
23	New Hampshire	3	13	23.1%
24	Kansas	7	31	22.6%
25	Hawaii	2	9	22.2%
25	South Carolina	10	45	22.2%
27	Iowa	6	29	20.7%
28	Delaware	1	5	20.0%
29	Oregon	6	30	20.0%
30	Oklahoma	7	36	19.4%

Rank	State	Number of A Hospitals	Number of Graded Hospitals	Percent (%) of A Hospitals
31	Nebraska	3	16	18.8%
32	Minnesota	7	38	18.4%
33	Washington	8	44	18.2%
34	New York	25	140	17.9%
35	Alabama	7	42	16.7%
36	Connecticut	4	25	16.0%
37	Indiana	9	59	15.3%
38	Mississippi	5	33	15.2%
39	Nevada	3	20	15.0%
40	Missouri	8	62	12.9%
41	Arkansas	3	26	11.5%
42	Montana	1	9	11.1%
42	Rhode Island	1	9	11.1%
44	West Virginia	2	24	8.3%
45	Alaska	0	5	0.0%
45	District of Columbia	0	7	0.0%
45	North Dakota	0	6	0.0%
45	New Mexico	0	16	0.0%
45	Vermont	0	6	0.0%
45	Wyoming	0	5	0.0%

http://www.hospitalsafetyscore.org/your-hospitals-safety-score/state-rankings

The Medical Bills
Did you know you can also negotiate the payment and pricing for your bill with any healthcare provider? Call and ask them what the discounted amount would be if you paid in full today.

Here are seven tips from experts on how to handle a hefty hospital bill:

1. Get organized. As soon as you're handed your first bill, be meticulous about keeping track of every one you receive. You may want to create a spreadsheet. There could be many bills — from the hospital, an assortment of doctors, the lab and the ambulance that took you to the medical center. Some won't come from the hospital itself, but from the particular provider that performed a service.

Don't hesitate to call the hospital-billing department to double check on charges you haven't seen yet but know you'll need to pay.

2. Vigilantly review the bills. Candice Butcher, vice president of Medical Billing Advocates of America, says if you're discharged in the morning (as most patients are), protest if you're socked with a full daily-room rate for the date you left the hospital.

And if you brought your medications with you, make sure you weren't charged for them by the hospital. "This frequently happens," Butcher says.

Also, dispute any additional fees on the bill for routine supplies, like gowns, gloves or sheets. These items should be factored into the hospital daily-room charge, because, Butcher says, they are "considered the cost of doing business."

3. Challenge your health insurer's decisions, when warranted. Keep track of any hospital bills the company rejects on grounds that the procedure or drug isn't covered by your policy. If you believe the insurer should be paying more, don't hesitate to appeal its decisions. You'd be surprised how often carriers overturn their earlier rejections.

4. Negotiate bills once you know how much you'll have to pay out of pocket. If you just want extra time to send the money, conversely you may be able to wrangle a cash discount for agreeing to pay your entire cost at once.

You may also be able to successfully bargain down the particular dollar amounts you've been charged.

Tell the billing department that if your insurance requires, say, a 20% co-payment to the hospital, you'll pay only 20% of the insurer's negotiated rate with that hospital. That's usually far less than the initial rate quoted — the figure charged to uninsured patients.Go online to check the rates other local hospitals charge for the procedure you had. Then, if you find your bill was way out of line, use this data as ammunition to try to get your fees lowered. You can get this type of information at such sites as Clear Health Costs, Healthcare Blue Book and FAIR Health.

Also consider using Medicare rates as a guide; the federal health system for people 65 and older typically has the lowest reimbursement rate for hospitals and medical providers. Your hospital may not agree to charge you its Medicare fee, but this figure is a good starting point for any negotiation.

5. Consider hiring a pro. Since hospital bills are hairy, messy beasts, it may be worth your while to bring in a patient- or medical-billing advocate or an attorney. Be sure you won't be required to pay this expert any fees upfront. Patient advocates typically charge 20 to 30% of your savings; some put a cap on their fees.

6. Find out if you're eligible for hospital financial assistance. You may be required to go through the rigmarole of applying for Medicaid and being rejected before the facility will provide its assistance, though.

7. Explore alternative fundraising. Many patients facing exorbitant hospital bills (and their families) have begun turning to crowd funding websites as a last-resort way of raising money to help cover their expenses. Sites for this strategy include:

GiveForward.com, GoFundMe.com, YouCaring.com, FundRazr.com
http://www.forbes.com/sites/nextavenue/2013/09/17/you-got-a-10000-hospital-bill-now-what/#28c60bb25fd0

Skilled Nursing Facility

The regulations surrounding the SNF, or Sniff as it is commonly called in the world of healthcare, is strict as well. Your loved one may not even be a candidate for rehab,but will be placed in a skilled nursing facility for up to up to 100 days. The SNF will typically use all of those days because Medicare and/or private insurance pays for this stay. You may receive little warning with regards to the discharge from services and you must take your loved one home or move them elsewhere. All of a sudden, your peace of mind goes out the door and you are faced with either making your home appropriate for them or you have to find a place to house them quickly.

Short-Term Recovery Care

Medicare covers most admissions to skilled nursing facilities (nursing homes) for patients recovering after a hospital stay. As long as a patient continues to be eligible, Medicare pays 100% of the eligible expenses for the first 20 days, and all but $133.50 a day (2009 amount) for up to 80 more days. If the patient is covered under a Medicare HMO, or has a Medicare Supplemental insurance policy (except Plan A or B), that plan will pay the $133.50 a day for as long as they continue to be eligible for coverage, up to the 80-day maximum. (But, on average, Medicare discharges patients after just 23 days of care in total.)

Long-Term Custodial Care

Contrary to the belief of most seniors, Medicare pays nothing for long-term care. It doesn't matter if the care is provided at home, in an assisted living facility, or in a nursing home.

Perhaps the confusion arises because Medicare can temporarily pay for nursing home care for recovering patients, as described in the section above. But, after they've recovered, Medicare's benefits stop even though the patient may remain in the nursing home as a permanent long-term resident.

Medicaid currently pays nearly half of all nursing home expenses. However, Medicaid reduces a senior's options to just one — a Medicaid nursing home with at least one roommate (no privacy). If local homes are full, the senior goes wherever a bed is available, even if it is hours away from family and friends. While no one really knows how this affects people with advanced Alzheimer's or senility, it can be devastating for an elderly person who is very frail but still mentally alert.

http://www.aging-parents-and-elder-care.com/Pages/Checklists

https://www.marinhhs.org/sites/default/files/files/servicepages/2013_07/ombudsman_skilled_nursing_facility_checklist.pdf

Find your State Skilled Nursing Facility below:

http://www.skillednursingfacilities.org/resources/medicare-quality-data/

You can find information about Skilled Nursing Facilities in your area at the link below:

https://www.medicare.gov/nursinghomecompare/search.html

https://www.cms.gov/Medicare/Provider-Enrollment-and-Certification/GuidanceforLawsAndRegulations/index.html

Skilled Nursing Facility Checklist

General Atmosphere
- Is the facility clean and relatively free of odors?
- Is the facility maintained at a comfortable temperature for patients?
- Are halls reasonably uncluttered?
- Are the Administrator and Director of nursing visible in the patient care areas?
- Is there a noticeable attitude of caring expressed toward the patients by all of the staff?
- Do the patients communicate with each other?
- Are visitors welcome?

Quality of Care
- Does the patient or his/her family participate in developing the patients care plan?
- Do the patients look well taken care of? (Are they dressed for the season and time of day?)
- Do patients who need assistance with eating receive it?
- Does staff respond quickly to patient calls for assistance?
- Is water readily available and are patients offered assistance in drinking water on a regular basis?

Patient's Rights
- Is privacy assured when the patients receive care?
- Are patients treated with dignity and respect?
- Are call bells placed within the patient's reach?
- Is an effort made to provide for roommate compatibility?
- Is there a program to restrict the use of physical restraints?

Staff
- Is the relationship between staff and residents warm, polite and respectful?
- Does staff wear name tags?
- Does the facility offer training and continuing education programs for all staff?
- Does the same team of nurses and Certified Nursing Assistants (CNA's) work with the same resident on an on-going basis?
- Is there a full-time social worker on staff?

Dietary
- Is a menu posted, and is it adhered to?
- Are meals hot and attractively served?
- Are fresh fruit and vegetables used in season?
- Are personal food likes and dislikes considered in meal planning?

Activity Program
- Is the calendar posted for the current month?
- Do activities take place as scheduled?
- Are there a variety of activities and do they seem to meet the patients' needs?
- Is there an activity plan for every patient, including room-bound and disoriented patients?

Chapter 4
A NEW HOME

Independent senior living communities, also known as retirement communities, senior living communities or independent retirement communities, are housing designed for seniors 55 and older.

Independent senior living communities commonly provide apartments, but some also offer cottages, condominiums, and single-family homes. Residents are seniors who do not require assistance with daily activities or 24/7 skilled nursing but may benefit from convenient services, senior-friendly surroundings, and increased social opportunities that independent senior living communities offer. Independent senior living communities are also popular among snowbird seniors who wish to downsize or travel freely without the burden of managing a home.

Many retirement communities offer dining services, basic housekeeping and laundry services, transportation to appointments and errands, activities, social programs, and access to exercise equipment. Some also offer emergency alert systems, live-in managers, and amenities like pools, spas, clubhouses, and on-site beauty and barber salons.

Independent senior living properties do not provide health care or assistance with activities of daily living (ADLs) such as medication, bathing, eating, dressing, toileting and more. Independent senior living differs from continuing care communities, which offer independent living along with multiple other levels of care, such as assisted living and skilled nursing, in one single residence.

The state does not monitor or regulate these types of communities and if you should run into an issue living there, you would have to address it with an attorney or state governing body for apartment communities.

On the following page is a listing of the type, characteristics and regulating body (if any) of this type of housing arrangement. You can also read more about it at the link below.

http://rcfereform.org/Who_Regulates_Independent_Living_Anybody

Independent Housing At A Glance

Housing Type	Characteristics	Regulated by
Low-Income Senior Housing	Subsidized HUD Housing Privately Owned but with HUD Contract Must be 62+ Offers no care or supervision Usually small apartment with kitchen, bathroom, and living room. Landlord/Tenant Law	U S Department of Housing & Urban Development (HUD) Applicable city ordinances
Senior Apartment Complexes or Mobile Home Parks	Privately Owned Usually 55+ No Care or Supervision Landlord/Tenant Law	Not Regulated - private businesses City Business licenses usually required Applicable city ordinances
Single Family Homes Converted for Senior Boarders	Privately owned Residential setting Rent a Bedroom with community bathrooms and kitchen privledges	Not Regulated - private businesses City Business licenses usually required Applicable city ordinances
Indpendent Living as part of RCFE*	Independent Living (IL) but with care and supervision available to be provided in the IL unit	Licensed by California Department of Social Services/Community Care Licensing *UNDER* the RCFE license. Regulated as an assisted living unit.
Indpendent Living as part of CCRC+	Independent Living (IL) but with care and supervision available to be provided in the IL unit as part of the continuing care compoent of the life-contract.	Licensed by California Department of Social Services/Community Care Licensing *UNDER* the RCFE license. Regulated as an assisted living unit.

* Residential Care Facility for the Elderly (RCFE)
\+ Continuing Care Retirement Community (includes Life contracts and Month to Month)

An **Assisted Living Facility** is a higher care place for those who have the need for medical assistance. They are required to be licensed in the state they operate in and are regulated by that state. These communities or facilities have medication technicians and personal care assistants at an additional fee cost which is added to your monthly rent. There is sometimes state financial assistance available and these types of communities can be either private pay or a combination of both.

Be aware that there typically is a nurse (LPN) available during daylight hours but is not heavily monitored. You will be reliant on the medical technicians (Med Tech) to be diligent with your delivery of medications and there is an additional cost associated to that service as well. Assisted Living facilities are regulated to some degree by the state, so check with your state of residency to find out what rules and laws they must abide by.

Senior Placement Services are typically paid for by the communities they represent. For instance, you see advertisements for "A Place for Mom" on television which charges a fee to the facility or community in exchange for an individual or couple moving in to live there. There are many placement service companies out there so be sure you speak with several and find the one you feel most comfortable with before moving forward.

APS – Adult Protective Services is a mandated program set forth to protect adults and seniors in unsafe or abusive environments. Regardless of where your loved one resides, anyone can place a call to APS even if they live at home with their family and file a complaint.

APS will investigate and follow up with the outcome of the investigation but this does not happen timely. The key with calling APS is that the person should be in danger, not a mere squabble within the family.

More resources:

National Center for Assisted Living website offers you a list by state of Assisted Living Facilities

https://www.ahcancal.org/ncal/resources/pages/assistedlivingregulations.aspx

Eldercare Locator is a government service link which offers resources and the ability to check for services and communities in your area by state. Please see the link below for your specific needs.

http://www.eldercare.gov/Eldercare.NET/Public/Index.aspx

Chapter 5

HOSPICE EXPLAINED

Palliative versus Hospice

Hospice is palliative which means relieving the pain and symptom control for a terminal illness of a person, but palliative care is not necessarily hospice because it allows curative treatment and is for any age person. See below.

Hospice is:

- Hospice is a special concept of care designed to provide comfort and support to patients and their families when a life-limiting illness no longer responds to cure-oriented treatments
- Hospice care neither prolongs life nor hastens death.
- Hospice staff and volunteers offer a specialized knowledge of medical care, including pain management.
- The goal of hospice care is to improve the quality of a patient's last days by offering comfort and dignity.
- Hospice care is provided by a team-oriented group of specially trained professionals, volunteers and family members.
- Hospice addresses all symptoms of a disease, with a special emphasis on controlling a patient's pain and discomfort.
- Hospice deals with the emotional, social and spiritual impact of the disease on the patient and the patient's family and friends.
- Hospice offers a variety of bereavement and counseling services to families before and after a patient's death.

Palliative is:

- Multidisciplinary approach to specialized medical care for people with serious illnesses
- It focuses on providing patients with relief from the symptoms, pain, physical stress, and mental stress of a serious illness—whatever the diagnosis.
- The goal of such therapy is to improve quality of life for patient
- It is provided by a team of physicians, nurses, and other health professionals who work together with the primary care

- physician and referred specialists to provide an extra layer of support
- It is appropriate at any age and at any stage in a serious illness and can be provided as the main goal of care or along with curative treatment.
- Palliative care can be provided across multiple settings including in hospitals, in the patient's home, as part of community palliative care programs, and in skilled nursing facilities.

What is hospice exactly?

Hospice is not a place but a service wherever the patient resides. It could be in an assisted living facility, a person's home, the adult child's home, an independent living community, a group home or even a box on the side of the road for a homeless Veteran. It is wherever the person resides.

Hospice is not a 24-hour service as some people often think. It is additional eyes and ears on the patient and gives "palliative" or comfort measures at the end of life which is 6 months or less preceding death.

Hospice is the next level of care that treats the **entire family** or anyone associated with the patient, not just the patient alone, unlike home health or rehabilitation services like physical therapy. The Center for Medicare Services (CMS) states that a person must have a terminal diagnosis which would cause them to pass within 6 months or less. It is not curative like home health services and doesn't seek curative treatment such as physical therapy, chemotherapy, radiation and the like.

Hospice does continue beyond the 6-month timeframe but the patient must be re-certified as terminally ill and this must be signed off by the physician who is the medical director of that hospice company

Hospice - You do have a choice with providers. Many times when the word hospice is brought up people panic and feel a sense of doom because they are faced with the finality and impending death of their loved one.   Their entire world changes and they rely on the expertise of the medical community to guide them during their time of crisis.   Here it explains that all persons have a "right to choose their provider" for any and all medical services.   Don't expect the doctor to explain hospice to you but he/she may refer you directly to a specific hospice company.

The doctor may have a relationship with a particular hospice company.   That physician may be the medical director or assistant medical director for that hospice company, they may have or know someone who works there.   Just know that you have a choice of providers for hospice and it's best to have 2 or 3 differing companies to review.

These are your rights under the Social Security Act of
SEC. 1802. [42 U.S.C. 1395a]

(a) BASIC FREEDOM OF CHOICE. —Any individual entitled to insurance benefits under this title may obtain health services from any institution, agency, or person qualified to participate under this title if such institution, agency, or person undertakes to provide him such services.
https://www.ssa.gov/OP_Home/ssact/title18/1802.htm

You will hear the term terminal diagnosis which is directly related to what illness they are dying from such as cancer, kidney (renal) failure, liver disease, hepatitis C, Congestive Heart Failure (CHF), and Chronic Obstructive Pulmonary Disease (COPD), Alzheimer's, and many more.   There is a complete list following this paragraph for a better understanding.   Within the diagnosis there are qualifiers and other factors involved as well to ensure the patient is truly a hospice candidate.   This was put in place for the protection of the patient and system itself.   Over the past few years there have been many companies fined millions of dollars for Medicare fraud related to hospice patients not being qualified for end of life services.   This is why it is critical that you request to speak with more than one Hospice Company.

YOUR HOSPICE TEAM INCLUDES:

You and your family members are the most important part of a team that may also include:

- Doctors
- Nurses or nurse practitioners
- Counselors
- Social workers
- Physical and occupational therapists
- Speech-language pathologists
- Hospice aides
- Homemakers
- Volunteers

Multidisciplinary Team of Experts

In addition, a hospice nurse and doctor are on-call 24 hours a day, 7 days a week to give you and your family support and care when you need it. A hospice doctor is part of your medical team. You can also choose to include your regular doctor or a nurse practitioner on your medical team, as the attending medical professional who supervises your care. The hospice benefit allows you and your family to stay together in the comfort of your home, unless you need care in an inpatient facility. If your hospice provider determines that you need inpatient hospice care, your hospice provider will make the arrangements for your stay

HOSPICE QUALIFIERS

- Alzheimer's Disease
- Amyotrophic Lateral Sclerosis (ALS) – check with CMS
- Cancer
- Cerebral Vascular Accident (CVA), Stroke & Coma
- Heart Disease/Congestive Heart Failure
- HIV Disease
- Huntington's Disease – check with CMS
- Liver Disease/Failure
- Lung Disease/COPD
- Multiple Sclerosis
- Muscular Dystrophy
- Myasthenia Gravis – check with CMS
- Parkinson's Disease – End Stage
- Renal Failure – Chronic
- Acquired Immune Deficiency Syndrome/HIV

Co-morbidities

You may here this term which means there may be additional conditions, as well as the main qualifying condition for hospice services. Although it may not be the primary hospice diagnosis, the presence of disease(s) such as the following, the severity of which is likely to contribute to a life expectancy of six months or less, should be considered in determining hospice eligibility.

- Chronic obstructive pulmonary disease
- Congestive heart failure
- Ischemic heart disease
- Diabetes mellitus
- Neurologic disease (CVA, ALS, MS, Parkinson's)
- Renal failure
- Liver Disease
- Neoplasia
- Acquired immune deficiency syndrome
- Dementia
- Refractory severe autoimmune disease (e.g. Lupus or Rheumatoid Arthritis)
- Inanition/Malnutrition

Levels of Hospice Services

The below listing is the services that Medicare requires each hospice to offer as a Condition of Participation for any hospice company.

Routine Home Care – happens in the home or where the person lives

Respite – requested by the Caregiver as a break, paid for 100% by Medicare and is a 5-day stay (only 5 days) in a Skilled Nursing Facility

GIP – General Inpatient – is done in a Skilled Nursing Facility for Symptoms out of control and is paid for 100% by Medicare until the Symptoms are manageable and the patient returns to their previous environment

Continuous Care – Provided during brief periods of crisis in the home. A continuous home care day is a day on which an individual who has elected to receive hospice care is not in an inpatient facility and receives hospice care consisting predominantly of nursing care on a continuous basis at home.

Home health aide or homemaker services or both may also be provided on a continuous basis. Continuous home care is only furnished during brief periods of crisis and only as necessary to maintain the terminally ill patient at home.

What Services Are Mandated by the Medicare Hospice Benefit?

Interdisciplinary Team of Hospice Professionals | Home Medical Equipment | Medication | Respite Care

Continuous Care | Inpatient Care | Routine Home Care | Bereavement Support

DISEASE TRAJECTORY

On the following page is a chart outlining the path and decline based on the acute diagnosis.

Rapid decline - these are typically Cancer patients and usually already on or referred to a hospice program.

- Progressive deterioration while receiving optimum appropriate care
- Increased hospitalization, ER or other health care services utilization
- Nutritional decline, functional decline
- Cancer- usual progression that ends in steady decline until death

Saw-tooth decline – Non Cancer diagnosis, [periodic crisis as opposed to frequent hospitalization, etc.
- COPD
- CHF
- Other organ system failures (liver, renal, etc.)
- Slow incremental decline with episodes of exacerbations
- Never really gets back to previous baseline

Slow Insidious decline – Lingering illnesses

- Dementia
- Stroke
- Parkinson's
- Other neurological illnesses
- Steady, slow progression leading to death

HOSPICE PATIENTS – DISEASE TRAJECTORIES

RAPID DECLINE
- Cancer

SAW-TOOTHED DECLINE
- Organ system failures (COPD, Heart Failure, etc.)

SLOW INSIDIOUS DECLINE
- Neurodegenerative disorders
- Dementia
- Debility

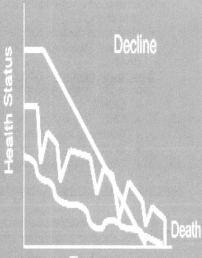

Resource: Field MJ, Cassel CK (eds), Institute of Medicine. Approaching Death: Improving Care at the End-of-life. Washington, DC: National Academy Press, 1997

A representative of the hospice company will come to you at your home and explain the services at no cost. It is at that time you should ask the following questions:

- How many locations do you have?
- Are you a regional, local or national hospice company?
- Can I meet your clinical staff?
- How quickly can my loved one get on services
- are you a non-profit or for profit company - this is tricky because non-profit doesn't mean they don't make money but it does mean they have a charity based program which helps when people have little to no funding options available
- What services are available through your company
- Do you offer a volunteer?
- What medications & medical equipment do you provide

FUNDING FOR HOSPICE SERVICES:

This is paid for by Medicare, Medicaid or private insurance companies but if there is no payer source there are charitable divisions of some hospices that help pay for those who have no funding source. Check with your local hospice companies and ask them about indigent services.

INTERDISCIPLINARY TEAM

The clinical team is known as the Interdisciplinary team or group. They typically meet bi-weekly to go over each patient status and updates and may also re-certify a patient for hospice services as a regulatory requirement at that time. It is during this meeting that the patient is discussed, the decline, the Medications, psycho social needs of the entire family, spiritual needs and much more. This is a requirement of Medicare funded hospice companies and all patients must have the appropriate medical documentation continually backing up the need for end of life services.

What Medicare covers

You can get a one-time only hospice consultation with a hospice medical director or hospice doctor to discuss your care options and management of your pain and symptoms. You can get this one-time consultation even if you decide not to get hospice care.

Medicare will cover the hospice care you get for your terminal illness and related conditions, but the care you get must be from a Medicare-approved hospice provider.

Important: Once you choose hospice care, the Medicare hospice benefit should cover everything you need. Original Medicare will still pay for covered benefits for any health problems that aren't part of your terminal illness and related conditions, but this is very rare.

Hospice care is usually given in your home. Depending on your terminal illness and related conditions, the plan of care your hospice team creates can include any or all of these services:

- Doctor services
- Nursing care
- Medical equipment (like wheelchairs or walkers)
- Medical supplies (like bandages and catheters)
- Prescription drugs
- Hospice aide and homemaker services
- Physical and occupational therapy
- Speech-language pathology services
- Social worker services
- Dietary counseling
- Grief and loss counseling for you and your family
- Short-term inpatient care (for pain and symptom management)
- Short-term respite care

Any other Medicare-covered services needed to manage your terminal illness and related conditions, as recommended by your hospice team

Respite care – covered by Medicare
If your usual caregiver (like a family member) needs a rest, you can get inpatient respite care in a Medicare-approved facility (like a hospice inpatient facility, hospital, or nursing home). Your hospice provider will arrange this for you. You can stay up to 5 days each time you get respite care. You can get respite care more than once, but it can only be provided on an occasional basis.

What the Medicare hospice benefit won't cover
When you choose hospice care, you've decided that you no longer want care to cure your terminal illness and related conditions, and/or your doctor has determined that efforts to cure your illness aren't working. Medicare won't cover any of these once you choose hospice care:

Treatment intended to cure your terminal illness and/or related conditions. Talk with your doctor if you're thinking about getting treatment to cure your illness. You always have the right to stop hospice care at any time. **Prescription drugs** (except for symptom control or pain relief).

Care from any provider that wasn't set up by the hospice medical team. You must get hospice care from the hospice provider you chose. All care that you get for your terminal illness and related conditions must be given by or arranged by the hospice team. You can't get the same type of hospice care from a different provider, unless you change your hospice provider. However, you can still see your regular doctor if you've chosen him or her to be the attending medical professional who helps supervise your hospice care.

Room and board. Medicare doesn't cover room and board. However, if the hospice team determines that you need short-term inpatient or respite care services that they arrange, Medicare will cover your stay in the facility. You may have to pay a small copayment for the respite stay.

Care you get as a hospital outpatient (like in an emergency room), care you get as a hospital inpatient, or ambulance transportation, unless it's either arranged by your hospice team or is unrelated to your terminal illness and related conditions.

Note: Contact your hospice team **before** you get any of these services, or you might have to pay the entire cost.

Chapter 6
VETERANS BENEFITS

Veteran's Benefits – It is key to understand that there are many services available to Veterans and spouse's/family members of Veterans. The initial issue is to make sure the Veteran has registered for benefits in the first place. Home Health, Hospice and Rehabilitative services are available through the Veteran's Benefits program. There are many qualifiers involved so it is best to contact your local Veteran representative, set a time to meet with them and let them explain and help you get started.

Check to see if the Hospice provider you are considering for your loved one participates with the "We Honor Veterans" program specifically designed for healthcare to Veterans.

http://www.wehonorveterans.org/partner-directory

Caregiver(s) that are family can receive assistance from the V.A. for caring for their Veteran loved one. Even while on hospice the V.A. offers a 30-day Respite service which allows the caregiver to use 30 days (set in hours) of time to have a local V.A. volunteer come stay with your loved one while you go out to run errands and such. Check with your local VA chapter representative to see if this service is available in your area. It does differ from the standard Respite care of hospice services. Hospice benefits paid for by the V.A. follows the same standards as Medicare regulations for hospice. It is typically the payer source when the person is under 65 and doesn't yet have Medicare benefits in place.

There are many different programs available to Veterans based on the geographical locations which includes homeless Veterans as well. The most important aspect is to speak with someone from the V.A., explain your situation and ask what "all" services are available to you and your family. For more information, please see links on the following page.

http://www.benefits.va.gov/benefits/
http://www.benefits.va.gov/PERSONA/veteran-homeless.asp
https://www.caregiver.org/faq-caregiving-veteran

Federal Benefits for Veterans, Dependents and Survivors

Phone Numbers	Office
Bereavement Counseling	1-202-461-6530
Civilian Health and Medical Program (CHAMPVA)	1-800-733-8387
Foreign Medical Program	1-888-820-1756
Headstones and Markers	1-800-697-6947
Health Care	1-877-222-8387
Homeless veterans	1-877-222-8387
Life Insurance	1-800-669-8477
National Cemetery Scheduling Office	1-800-535-1117
Pension Management Center	1-877-294-6380
Presidential Memorial Certificate Program	1-202-565-4964
Special Health Issues	1-800-749-8387
Telecommunication Device for the Deaf (TDD)	1-800-829-4833
VA Benefits	1-800-827-1000
Women Veterans	1-202-461-1070

Chapter 7
Other legal services

Fiduciary services - A **fiduciary** is a person who holds a legal or ethical relationship of trust with one or more other parties (person or group of persons). The local county usually has a judiciary service for those individuals who have no surviving family members and they are entrusted with the moral and legal responsibility to get the correct services for the person they represent.

Medical Power of Attorney – You will want to get a Medical or Durable Power of Attorney signed by your loved one prior to them becoming severely ill, so that you can make the appropriate decisions for them when they can no longer make it for themselves. It is critical to have this document in order to provide the best services and the best person to handle this is the person who will abide by the wishes of the patient or ill person, not necessarily a family member or loved one.

http://www.americanbar.org/content/dam/aba/administrative/law_aging/2011/2011_aging_hcdec_univhcpaform_4_2012_v2.authcheckdam.pdf

Some states allow you to print this form off of the internet and require a two-person witness for signatures and/or a Notary Public. Check your local state to see if you can do this without hiring an attorney. It may also be called an Advanced Directive form.

DNR – Do Not Resuscitate is a form that is highly recommended when a person is on hospice services but it is not required to receive hospice.
Simply stated, if you do not want to prolong your life in the event of a catastrophic or terminal illness, then you want a DNR on file.

The next few pages will explain these helpful tools in detail.

What is an advance directive?

An advance directive tells your doctor what kind of care you would like to have if you become unable to make medical decisions (if you are in a coma, for example). If you are admitted to the hospital, the hospital staff will probably talk to you about advance directives.

A good advance directive describes the kind of treatment you would want depending on how sick you are. For example, the directives would describe what kind of care you want if you have an illness that you are unlikely to recover from, or if you are permanently unconscious. Advance directives usually tell your doctor that you don't want certain kinds of treatment. However, they can also say that you want a certain treatment no matter how ill you are.

Advance directives can take many forms. Laws about advance directives are different in each state. You should be aware of the laws in your state.

What is a living will?
A living will is one type of advance directive. It is a written, legal document that describes the kind of medical treatments or life-sustaining treatments you would want if you were seriously or terminally ill. A living will doesn't let you select someone to make decisions for you.

What is a durable power of attorney for health care?
A durable power of attorney (DPA) for health care is another kind of advance directive. A DPA states whom you have chosen to make health care decisions for you. It becomes active any time you are unconscious or unable to make medical decisions. A DPA is generally more useful than a living will. But a DPA may not be a good choice if you don't have another person you trust to make these decisions for you.

Living wills and DPAs are legal in most states. Even if these advance directives aren't officially recognized by the law in your state, they can still guide your loved ones and doctor if you are unable to make decisions about your medical care. Ask your doctor, lawyer or state representative about the law in your state.

What is a Do Not Resuscitate (DNR) order?

A do not resuscitate (DNR) order is another kind of advance directive. A DNR is a request not to have cardiopulmonary resuscitation (CPR) if your heart stops or if you stop breathing. Unless given other instructions, hospital staff will try to help any patient whose heart has stopped or who has stopped breathing. You can use an advance directive form or tell your doctor that you don't want to be resuscitated. Your doctor will put the DNR order in your medical chart. Doctors and hospitals in all states accept DNR orders.

Should I have an advance directive?

By creating an advance directive, you are making your preferences about medical care known before you're faced with a serious injury or illness. This will spare your loved ones the stress of making decisions about your care while you are sick. Any person 18 years of age or older can prepare an advance directive.

People who are seriously or terminally ill are more likely to have an advance directive. For example, someone who has terminal cancer might write that she does not want to be put on a respirator if she stops breathing. This action can reduce her suffering, increase her peace of mind and increase her control over her death. However, even if you are in good health, you might want to consider writing an advance directive. An accident or serious illness can happen suddenly, and if you already have a signed advance directive, your wishes are more likely to be followed.

How can I write an advance directive?

You can write an advance directive in several ways:

- Use a form provided by your doctor.
- Write your wishes down by yourself.
- Call your health department or state department on aging to get a form
- Call a lawyer.
- Use a computer software package for legal documents.

Advance directives and living wills do not have to be complicated legal documents. They can be short, simple statements about what you want done or not done if you can't speak for yourself. Remember, anything you write by yourself or with a computer software package should follow your state laws. You may also want to have what you have written reviewed by your doctor or a lawyer to make sure your directives are understood exactly as you intended. When you are satisfied with your directives, the orders should be notarized if possible, and copies should be given to your family and your doctor.

Can I change my advance directive?
You may change or cancel your advance directive at any time, as long as you are considered of sound mind to do so. Being of sound mind means that you are still able to think rationally and communicate your wishes in a clear manner. Again, your changes must be made, signed and notarized according to the laws in your state. Make sure that your doctor and any family members who knew about your directives are also aware that you have changed them.

If you do not have time to put your changes in writing, you can make them known while you are in the hospital. Tell your doctor and any family or friends present exactly what you want to happen. Usually, wishes that are made in person will be followed in place of the ones made earlier in writing. Be sure your instructions are clearly understood by everyone you have told.

Chapter 8

THE IMPORTANCE OF LIFE INSURANCE

We hear about purchasing life insurance all the time, especially if you are over 50 years of age. I have and do recommend a policy to help cover funeral and burial expenses. You may also choose to have a larger policy to ensure your living loved ones have extra to support their needs after your death. It is important to meet with an insurance advisor you trust and almost all insurance companies sell policies.

Whether to choose a Whole Life policy or a Term policy is entirely up to you. I won't go in to detail about this decision but I do believe it is vital to those living family members left behind so that the financial burden of your burial and memorial services, if any, aren't left to their budget. This can be a source of great debate and concern within family dynamics if there is no money to assist in burying their deceased loved one.

Just know that the older you are, the more expensive the life insurance will be for a monthly premium and term life insurance does have an expiration date when your payment will suddenly balloon in monthly premium. Get all the facts before you decide and then spend some money to assist for your departure from this earthly realm.

If your loved one was a Veteran, there may be benefits to help cover the cost of a funeral and memorial services. Check with your Veteran's Administration representative or call to see if they qualify.

While my parents didn't have large policies, they did make sure they had enough to cover their burial expenses and memorial services and I am very grateful for that.

This is a gift you give your loved ones so that they won't have to figure a way to pay for your expenses after you pass.

Chapter 9

BURIAL & FUNERAL SERVICES

Most people plan for funeral and burial services when their loved one passes. I've gone through this situation on three separate occasions and learned the best way to handle this is prior to the death of your loved one.

Ask your family what type of service they want. Do they want a memorial prior to the burial? Do you want a quick burial and have a memorial service afterwards? There is no right or wrong decision and you can handle this service in any manner of your choosing. Just keep in mind that the memorial service is for you, your friends and family and offers closure to those who didn't expect your loved one to pass, or were unaware of the impending death. Even if they were aware, this is a way to seek and fulfill closure for all those who befriended your loved one.

Research several different companies and ask for pricing prior to meeting with them or making a decision. If you are doing a traditional burial with a casket, then be sure and stay within your budget regardless of whether there is a life insurance premium or not. This is a highly emotional purchase so be sure that the entire family is involved. If you are opting for a cremation, then there are discounted programs for that as well.

Talk to your pastor or clergy man about services or a memorial for your loved one and if you can't afford that, you can always do this in your home or wherever you choose. Again, there is no right or wrong place to have a memorial service.

If your loved one is a Veteran, then they may have an "Honor Guard" available for the funeral or memorial services. Be sure and ask your representative at the Veteran's Administration about this beautiful ceremony in honor of your loved one who so graciously served our country.

The Death Certificate - you can get from the local coroner's office or the funeral home, but your loved one must be "pronounced deceased" and a doctor must sign off on it before you can get a death certificate. Be sure and ask for several certified death certificates as these will need to be presented for financial and personal reasons later.

Additionally, when your loved one passes should they have any outstanding debt, you are not responsible for it. For instance, my mother had a phone bill that was due and the representative tried to coerce me into paying it after she passed by stating, "Your mother had a perfect payment history, I'm sure you'd like to complete that for her now, wouldn't you?"

My response to this person was that I'm sure God didn't care about her debt now that she was in Heaven. Don't be bullied by debtors after your loved one has passed on. You'll have enough to deal with to just grieve your losses and you are not personally responsible for their debt as long as your name is not part of the debt arrangement.

Do make sure that you continue to allow yourself to grieve and hold as many memorials for as many years as you like to help you achieve your sense of closure. Grief is very personal and only you can determine how to handle your own feelings and emotions.

http://www.funeralhomedirectory.com/

http://www.legacy.com/funeral-homes/

Resource: http://www.cremationresource.org/cremation/how-to-decide-whether-to-cremate-or-bury.html

Chapter 10
MEDICAID VS. MEDICARE

Medicaid vs. Medicare

Medicaid is state assistance and it depends on if your state has the funding. For instance, Kansas did not buy into the federal program and has little to no funding for their Medicaid program. Arizona has a decent program for state health insurance program called AHCCCS or Arizona HealthCare Cost Containment System. In Arizona there is also low-income housing assistance through their ALTCS program, also known as Arizona Long Term Care System.

If you're loved one goes on state funding for housing assistance (ALTCS) they will have to give up all their assets to the state. In most cases, the family sells the house and uses this money for payment for assisted living and then once it dries up, they apply for funding by the state program. You MUST apply for state funding 6 months to a year prior to your liquid assets depleting. It takes that long for the process to go through all phases until finality. And there is no guarantee you will qualify or be awarded state assistance.

ALTCS which is state funding, does typically pay for housing/room & board. Medicare does not which is a common misconception among the general public. People sometimes think that Medicare pays for everything when, in fact, it is only the healthcare coverage portion which was funded from your employment as a citizen of the United States and paying into the Social Security & FICA funds. If you are not a citizen of the United States or recently became one, then you will only be qualified for Medicare Part B which covers medications and may have eligibility status for state funding assistance for your medical needs. It makes sense that if you have not paid taxes as a working citizen of the United States then you are not entitled to funding for services paid for by U.S. citizens.

Each state establishes and administers their own Medicaid state funded programs and determines the type, amount, duration, and scope of services within broad federal guidelines. States are required to cover

certain "mandatory benefits," and can choose to provide other "optional benefits" through the Medicaid program.

Medicaid has mandatory benefits listed in this chapter.   For a full list please see the link after the explanation of benefits.

- Inpatient hospital services
- Outpatient hospital services
- EPSDT: Early and Periodic Screening, Diagnostic, and Treatment Services
- Nursing Facility Services
- Home health services
- Physician services
- Rural health clinic services
- Federally qualified health center services
- Laboratory and X-ray services
- Family planning services
- Nurse Midwife services
- Certified Pediatric and Family Nurse Practitioner services
- Freestanding Birth Center services (when licensed or otherwise recognized by the state)
- Transportation to medical care
- Tobacco cessation counseling for pregnant women

> Medicare is the federally funded government program for people 65 and older which covers medically necessary services.   It can include rehabilitation, home health, hospice, hospital stay, skilled nursing facility stay and other services.   CMS, the Center for Medicare, is the governing body

and determines what will and will not be paid for based on regulations put forth by the federal government.

Medicare benefits are paid for by all working U.S. Citizens and taken from your paycheck each pay period. There has been a surge in investigations of hospice and home health companies because some have not abided by regulatory statutes. This is what Medicare deems fraud and it cost you and me, the taxpayers, more money with the increasing rise of healthcare costs.

Not to mention, it is basically stealing from each of us and those who paid in over the years. Taking money from those individuals who need and deserve the services.

MEDICARE PROGRAMS EXPLAINED

Many people think Medicare is an all-inclusive service paying for everything a person might need. Below is the breakdown on what is covered by the different parts of Medicare.

Different parts of Medicare cover different services. You may hear about four parts of Medicare: Part A, Part B, Part C, and Part D. Original Medicare is administered directly by the federal government, is the way most people get their Medicare, and has two parts:

1. **Part A** (Hospital Insurance) covers most medically necessary hospital, skilled nursing facility, home health, and hospice care. It is free if you have worked and paid Social Security taxes for at least 40 calendar quarters (10 years); you will pay a monthly premium if you have worked and paid taxes for less time.

2. **Part B** (Medical Insurance) covers most medically necessary doctors' services, preventive care, durable medical equipment, hospital outpatient services, laboratory tests, x-rays, mental health

care, and some home health and ambulance services. You pay a monthly premium for this coverage.

Medicare Part D (outpatient Prescription Drug Insurance) is the part of Medicare that provides outpatient prescription drug coverage. Part D is provided only through private insurance companies that have contracts with the government—it is never provided directly by the government (like Original Medicare is).

If you want Part D, you must choose Part D coverage that works with your Medicare health benefits. If you have Original Medicare, choose a stand-alone Part D plan (PDP).

Medicare Part C is not a separate benefit. Part C is the part of Medicare policy that allows private health insurance companies to provide Medicare benefits. These Medicare private health plans, such as HMOs and PPOs, are known as Medicare Advantage Plans. If you want, you can choose to get your Medicare coverage through a Medicare Advantage Plan instead of through Original Medicare.

Medicare Advantage Plans must offer at least the same benefits as Original Medicare (those covered under Parts A and B) but can do so with different rules, costs, and coverage restrictions. You also typically get Part D as part of your Medicare Advantage benefits package. Many different kinds of Medicare Advantage Plans are available. You may pay a monthly premium for this coverage, in addition to your Part B premium.

https://www.cms.gov/
http://oig.hhs.gov/fraud/report-fraud/
http://www.medicareinteractive.org/get-answers

Chapter 11

FAMILY GATHERING & THE TALK

Research the information and have the doctor or nurse present in the initial conversation, so that if clinical questions come up they can be addressed. Then have a similar conversation at home and always let the family behave the way that is best for them to cope.

The most important and difficult conversation you will have is the talk about your loved one's condition. Take special time out to visit and don't make light or jokes about the situation. Be honest and explain it in terms that everyone can understand, the less clinical the better. When explaining the condition be sure to think of everyone in the room as not having any knowledge about the topic and try to be as concise as possible.

Some family members cry, some get angry, some don't have any feelings and remain stoic. It is very individual with each person regarding their own reaction and processing of the illness of their loved one or themselves. Don't judge them just let them react and remain calm. Offer comfort if they want it but allow them their own personal space and their own way to grieve the news.

There is a book called "5 Wishes" which I highly recommend to all persons and families regardless of whether you have an illness or not. It helps plan and protect the family unit before the crisis arises.

The Five Wishes

Wishes 1 and 2 are both legal documents. Once signed, they meet the legal requirements for an advance directive in the states listed on the next page. Wishes 3, 4, and 5 are unique to Five Wishes, in that they address matters of comfort care, spirituality, forgiveness, and final wishes.

Wish 1: The Person I Want to Make Care Decisions for Me When I Can't

This section is an assignment of a health care agent (also called proxy, surrogate, representative, or health care power of attorney). This person makes medical decisions on your behalf if you are unable to speak for yourself.

Wish 2: The Kind of Medical Treatment I Want or Don't Want

This section is a living will—a definition of what life support treatment means to you, and when you would and would not want it.

Wish 3: How Comfortable I Want to Be

This section addresses matters of comfort care—what type of pain management you would like, personal grooming and bathing instructions, and whether you would like to know about options for hospice care, among others.

Wish 4: How I Want People to Treat Me

This section speaks to personal matters, such as whether you would like to be at home, whether you would like someone to pray at your bedside, among others.

Wish 5: What I Want My Loved Ones to Know

This section deals with matters of forgiveness, how you wish to be remembered, and final wishes regarding funeral or memorial plans.

5 Wishes Meets Legal Requirements in 42 States

According to analysis by the American Bar Association's Commission on Law and Aging. Five Wishes currently meets the legal requirements for an advance directive in the following 42 states and the District of Columbia. In the remaining 8 states, (Alabama, Indiana, Kansas, New Hampshire, Ohio, Oregon, Texas, and Utah) a statutory form is required, and one must attach the state document if one wishes to use the Five Wishes document as a guide.

Alaska	Arizona	Arkansas	California	Colorado
Connecticut	Delaware	Florida	Georgia	Hawaii
Idaho	Illinois	Iowa	Kentucky	Louisiana
Maine	Maryland	Massachusetts	Michigan	Minnesota
Mississippi	Missouri	Montana	Nebraska	Nevada
New Jersey	New Mexico	New York	North Carolina	North Dakota
Oklahoma	Pennsylvania	Rhode Island	South Carolina	South Dakota
Tennessee	Vermont	Virginia	Washington	West Virginia
Wisconsin	Wyoming			

Resource: https://agingwithdignity.org/

Chapter 12

THE STAGES OF GRIEF

The five stages, denial, anger, bargaining, depression and acceptance are a part of the framework that makes up our learning to live with the one we lost. They are tools to help us frame and identify what we may be feeling. But they are not stops on some linear timeline in grief. Not everyone goes through all of them or in a prescribed order. Our hope is that with these stages comes the knowledge of griefs terrain, making us better equipped to cope with life and loss. At times, people in grief will often report more stages. Just remember your grief is as unique as you are.

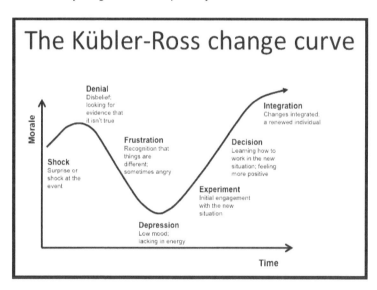

http://changingminds.org/disciplines/change_management/kubler_ross/kubler_ross.htm

STAGES OF GRIEF:

The stages of grief come in no particular order and can be experienced before, during and after loss for many years to come. However you experience grief, it is your normal.

DENIAL
Denial is the first of the five stages of grief. It helps us to survive the loss. In this stage, the world becomes meaningless and overwhelming. Life makes no sense. We are in a state of shock and denial. We go numb. We wonder how we can go on, if we can go on, why we should go on. We try to find a way to simply get through each day. Denial and shock help us to cope and make survival possible. Denial helps us to pace our feelings of grief. There is a grace in denial. It is nature's way of letting in only as much as we can handle. As you accept the reality of the loss and start to ask yourself questions, you are unknowingly beginning the healing process. You are becoming stronger, and the denial is beginning to fade. But as you proceed, all the feelings you were denying begin to surface.

ANGER
Anger is a necessary stage of the healing process. Be willing to feel your anger, even though it may seem endless. The more you truly feel it, the more it will begin to dissipate and the more you will heal. There are many other emotions under the anger and you will get to them in time, but anger is the emotion we are most used to managing. The truth is that anger has no limits. It can extend not only to your friends, the doctors, your family, yourself and your loved one who died, but also to God. You may ask, "Where is God in this? Underneath anger is pain, your pain. It is natural to feel deserted and abandoned, but we live in a society that fears anger. Anger is strength and it can be an anchor, giving temporary structure to the nothingness of loss. At first grief feels like being lost at sea: no connection to anything. Then you get angry at someone, maybe a person who didn't attend the funeral, maybe a person who isn't around, maybe a person who is different now that your loved one has died. Suddenly you have a structure – – your anger toward them. The anger becomes a bridge over the open sea, a connection from you to them. It is something to hold onto; and a connection made from the strength of anger feels better than nothing. We usually know more

about suppressing anger than feeling it. The anger is just another indication of the intensity of your love.

BARGAINING

Before a loss, it seems like you will do anything if only your loved one would be spared. "Please God," you bargain, "I will never be angry at my wife again if you'll just let her live." After a loss, bargaining may take the form of a temporary truce. "What if I devote the rest of my life to helping others." Then can I wake up and realize this has all been a bad dream?" We become lost in a maze of "If only…" or "What if…" statements. We want life returned to what is was; we want our loved one restored. We want to go back in time: find the tumor sooner, recognize the illness more quickly, stop the accident from happening…if only, if only, if only. Guilt is often bargaining's companion. The "if only" cause us to find fault in ourselves and what we "think" we could have done differently. We may even bargain with the pain. We will do anything not to feel the pain of this loss. We remain in the past, trying to negotiate our way out of the hurt. People often think of the stages as lasting weeks or months. They forget that the stages are responses to feelings that can last for minutes or hours as we flip in and out of one and then another. We do not enter and leave each individual stage in a linear fashion. We may feel one, then another and back again to the first one.

DEPRESSION

After bargaining, our attention moves squarely into the present. Empty feelings present themselves, and grief enters our lives on a deeper level, deeper than we ever imagined. This depressive stage feels as though it will last forever. It's important to understand that this depression is not a sign of mental illness. It is the appropriate response to a great loss. We withdraw from life, left in a fog of intense sadness, wondering, perhaps, if there is any point in going on alone. Why go on at all? Depression after a loss is too often seen as unnatural: a state to be fixed, something to snap out of. The first question to ask yourself is whether or not the situation you're in is actually depressing. The loss of a loved one is a very depressing situation, and depression is a normal and appropriate response. To not experience depression after a loved one dies would be unusual.

When a loss fully settles in your soul, the realization that your loved one didn't get better this time and is not coming back is understandably depressing. If grief is a process of healing, then depression is one of the many necessary steps along the way.

ACCEPTANCE

Acceptance is often confused with the notion of being "all right" or "OK" with what has happened. This is not the case. Most people don't ever feel OK or all right about the loss of a loved one. This stage is about accepting the reality that our loved one is physically gone and recognizing that this new reality is the permanent reality. We will never like this reality or make it OK, but eventually we accept it. We learn to live with it. It is the new norm with which we must learn to live. We must try to live now in a world where our loved one is missing. In resisting this new norm, at first many people want to maintain life as it was before a loved one died. In time, through bits and pieces of acceptance, however, we see that we cannot maintain the past intact. It has been forever changed and we must readjust. We must learn to reorganize roles, re-assign them to others or take them on ourselves. Finding acceptance may be just having more good days than bad ones. As we begin to live again and enjoy our life, we often feel that in doing so, we are betraying our loved one. We can never replace what has been lost, but we can make new connections, new meaningful relationships, new interdependencies. Instead of denying our feelings, we listen to our needs; we move, we change, we grow, we evolve. We may start to reach out to others and become involved in their lives. We invest in our friendships and in our relationship with ourselves. We begin to live again, but we cannot do so until we have given grief its time.

Your grief is as unique as you are and the above information about the stages and processes don't necessarily come in no particular order, but a pattern was established. So, you may vacillate back-and-forth between some or all of the stages, just know that is perfectly fine. It's you and your emotions not a set script. Be gentle on yourself.

Children Also Mourn

Mourning is the recognition of a deeply felt loss and a process we all must go through before we are able to pick up the pieces and go on living fully and normally again. Mourning heals. By being open with our sorrow and tears, we show our children that it is all right to feel sad and to cry. The expression of grief should never be equated with weakness. Our sons as well as our daughters should be allowed to shed their tears and express their feelings if and when they need to.

A child may show little immediate grief, and we may think she is unaffected by the loss. Some mental health experts believe that children are not mature enough to work through a deeply felt loss until they are adolescents. Because of this, they say, children are apt to express their sadness on and off over a long period of time and often at unexpected moments. Other family members may find it painful to have old wounds probed again and again, but children need patience, understanding, and support to complete their "grief work".

- Communication about death, as with all communication, is easier when a child feels that she has our permission to talk about the subject and believes we are sincerely interested in her views and questions. Encourage her to communicate by listening attentively, respecting her views, and answering her questions honestly.
- Every child is an individual. Communication about death depends on her age and her own experiences. If she is very young, she may view death as temporary, and she may be more concerned about separation from her loved ones than about death itself.
- It is not always easy to "hear" what a child is really asking. Sometimes it may be necessary to respond to a question with a question in order to fully understand the child's concern.
- A very young child can absorb only limited amounts of information. Answers need to be brief, simple, and repeated when necessary
- A child often feels guilty and angry when she loses a close family member. She needs reassurance that she has been, and will continue to be, loved and cared for.

- A child may need to mourn a deeply felt loss on and off until she is in her adolescence. She needs support and understanding through this grief process and permission to show her feelings openly and freely.
- Whether a child should visit the dying or attend a funeral depends on her age and ability to understand the situation, her relationship with the dying or dead person, and, most important, whether she wishes it.
- A child should never be coerced or made to feel guilty if she prefers not to be involved. If she is permitted to visit a dying person or attend a funeral, she should be prepared in advance for what she will hear and see.

NEEDS OF A GRIEVING CHILD:

- Information that is clear and understandable at their development level.
- to be reassured that their basic needs will be met.
- to be involved in planning for the funeral and anniversary
- to be reassured when grieving by adults is intense
- help with exploring fantasies about death, afterlife, and related issues.
- to be able to have and express their own thoughts and behaviors, especially when different from significant adults.
- to maintain age appropriate activities and interests.
- to receive help with "magical thinking."
- to say good-bye to the deceased.
- to memorialize the deceased.

Before the Death

- help with anticipatory grief
- to be given information about the physical, emotional, and mental condition of the terminally ill person and given a choice of visiting or remaining away.
- to be allowed to care for the dying person.
- to participate in meaningful ways of saying goodbye.
- to have schedules and boundaries as close to normal as possible.
- to receive affection and be listened to.

Signals for Attention from a Grieving Child

- marked change in school performance.
- poor grades despite trying very hard.
- A lot of worry or anxiety manifested by refusing to go to school, go to sleep, or take part in age appropriate activities.
- not talking about the person or the death. Physically avoiding mention of the deceased.
- frequent angry outbursts or anger expressed in destructive ways.
- hyperactive activities, fidgeting, constant movement beyond regular playing
- persistent anxiety or phobias.
- accident proneness, possibly self-punishment or a call for attention.
- persistent nightmares or sleeping disorders.
- stealing, promiscuity, vandalism, illegal behavior
- persistent disobedience or aggression (longer than six months) and violations of the rights of others.
- opposition to authority figures.
- frequent unexplainable temper tantrums.
- social withdrawal
- alcohol or other drug abuse.
- inability to cope with problems and daily activities
- many complaints of physical ailments
- persistent depression accompanied by poor appetite, sleep difficulties, and thoughts of death.
- long term absence of emotion
- frequent panic attacks
- persistent symptoms of the deceased.

Characteristics of Age Groups (to be used only as a general guide)

Infants - 2 Years Old:

- Will sense a loss
- Will pick up on grief of a parent or caretaker
- May change eating, sleeping, toilet habits.

2-6 Years Old:

- Family is center of child's world
- Confident family will care for her needs
- Plays grown-ups, imitates adults.
- Functions on a day-to-day basis.
- No understanding of time or death
- Cannot imagine life without mum or dad
- Picks up on nonverbal communication.
- Thinks dead people continue to do things (eat, drink, go to the bathroom), but only in the sky.
- Thinks if you walk on the grave the person feels it.
- Magical thinking
- you wish it, it happens (bring the dead back or wishing someone was dead)
- Death brings confusion, guilt [magically thought someone dead]
- Tendency to connect things which are not related.

6-9 Years Old:

- Personifies death: A person, monster who takes you away
- Sometimes a violent thing.
- Still has magical thinking, yet begins to see death as final, but outside the realm of the child's realistic mind.
- Fails to accept that death will happen to them - or to anyone (although begins to suspect that it will).
- Fears that death is something contagious.
- Confusion of wording [soul/sole, dead body, live soul].
- Develops an interest in the causes of death (violence, old age, sickness).

9-12-Year-Old:

- May see death as punishment for poor behavior.
- Develops morality - strong sense of good and bad behavior.
- Still some magical thinking.
- Needs reassurance that wishes do not kill.
- Begins an interest in biological factors of death.
- Theorizes: People die to make room for new people.
- Asks more about "what happened"

- Concerns about ritual, burying
- Questions relationship changes caused by death, life changes.
- Worries about who provides and cares for them.
- May regress to an earlier stage
- Interested in spiritual aspects of death.

Teenagers:

- Views death as inevitable, universal, irreversible.
- Cognitive skills developed
- Thinks like an adult
- Questions meaning of life if it ends in death
- Sees aging process leading to death
- Sees self as invincible - it will not happen to me.
- Sees death as a natural enemy
- Need for adult guidance (grief process, coping skills).
- Needs someone to listen; to talk with.
- May feel guilt, anger, even some responsibility for death that occurred.
- Not sure how to handle own emotions [public and private].

Resources:

http://grief.com/the-five-stages-of-grief/

https://en.wikipedia.org/wiki/K%C3%BCbler-Ross_model
http://changingminds.org/disciplines/change_management/kubler_ross/kubler_ross.htm

http://www.centering.org/img/BereavementGuideUPDATE8-31-2011.pdf

http://www.hospicenet.org/html/talking.html

Chapter 13

UNDERSTANDING THE CLINICAL SIDE

This brief chapter is dedicated to the clinical team of doctors, nurses and specialists in the field of medicine who are sometimes looked at as without heart.

If you think about it, doctors are trained to "cure" people and save lives but are taught very little about death and dying. When they've exhausted all their energy, education and resources they are left with a feeling of guilt, frustration and even personal failure. They've spent countless hours researching and trying to find a way to cure their patient and may have even become close to the patient and family. We can't fault most doctors because they truly do care and want to do what is in the best interest of the patient. This applies to nurses as well, however they tend to become more attached because they spend more one-on-one time with the patient and family and perform the "hands on" care.

I've met many clinical staff who compartmentalize their jobs so that they don't go home emotionally empty and suffer from depression. The world is all about life and living, but in the field of healthcare they deal with sickness and the dying. It's altruistic and can be very rewarding except when the news of impending death is given.

The greatest reward for a healthcare worker is knowing they have made a difference in someone's life. We tend to lean on physicians and nurses to be experts in the field of medicine when the reality is that each person is unique. We, as human beings are made up of a DNA structure making us similar yet the outcome of our lives and passing is as individual as the person.

Just remember that your healthcare provider whether it is the nurse, doctor, specialist, etc. is concerned about your health and well-being but they are only human and feel the weight of your concerns and issues long after you leave their office and care.

Chapter 14
CAREGIVER STRESS

Caregivers suffer extreme stress related to the care of their loved one, especially during the last stages of life. It demands odd hours and often allows no time for others in your life. Therefore, you must be the one to take care of yourself. The fear of what others think must be set aside when you are caring for yourself. Because you are the caregiver of another ask yourself these questions, if you answer yes to any of them, it is time for you to care for yourself.

- . Do I have trouble getting organized?
- . Do I cry for no reason?
- . Do I feel numb and emotionless?
- . Do I feel constantly pressed for time?
- . Am I short tempered?
- . Are everyday tasks getting harder to accomplish?
- . Do I feel that I just can't do anything right?
- . Do I feel that I have no time for myself?

It may seem impossible to take better care of yourself at this time, but read this list of suggestions below as guidelines and know that you must also care for yourself in order to continue to care for your loved one.

- Get enough rest by deciding how much you need and setting aside that amount of time.
- Read, listen to music, take a warm bath or shower to help you wind down. Take 10 minute breaks during the day.
- Eat well and at regular times.
- Eat foods from each of the food groups daily.
- Delegate tasks, especially if there is more than one person involved with the care. Allow the other caregiver some room to do the task in their own way and hire help if possible.
- Allow that friend or neighbor to help if they want to. Don't try to be a superhuman because you cannot do it all.
- Confide in someone - a family member, a close friend, a Social Worker, clergy, a support group. Talking about your loved one and dying does help.
- Allow yourself some quality time alone.

CAREGIVER STRESS RESOURCES:

Arizona Caregiver Coalition - http://azcaregiver.org

Warrior Care - http://warriorcare.dodlive.mil/caregiver-resources

National Caregivers Library -
http://www.caregiverslibrary.org/home.aspx

Caregiver Action Network –
http://caregiveraction.org/resources/agencies-and-organizations

Institute for Caregiving -
http://www.rosalynncarter.org/caregiver_resources

AARP –
https://www.aarp.org/caregiving/local/info-2017/important-resources-for-caregivers.html

National Alliance for Caregiving
http://www.caregiving.org/resources

Caregiving – Online learning course -
https://www.careandcompliance.com/caregivers-training-solutions/online-training/caregiver-certifications/caregiver-core-certification.html?gclid=EAlalQobChMlw76Fu_GY2glV1LfACh3J gg-AEAAYASAAEglgKPD_BwE

Arizona Dept. of Economic Security – Support for Caregivers
https://des.az.gov/services/aging-and-adult/support-caregivers/being-paid-be-family-caregiver

Area Agency on Aging – Caregiver resources

https://www.aaaphx.org/caring-for-someone/caring-resources

Chapter 15

DEMENTIA - Explained

DIFFERENT TYPES OF DEMENTIA
- Alzheimer's disease
- Vascular dementia
- Dementia with Lewy Bodies
- Mixed dementia
- Parkinson's disease
- Frontotemporal dementia
- Creutzfeldt-Jakob disease (Mad Cow diseases)
- Normal pressure hydrocephalus
- Huntington's disease
- Wernicke-Korsakoff syndrome

ALZHEIMER'S DISEASE

Alzheimer's is the most common type of dementia; accounts for an estimated 60 to 80 percent of cases.

Symptoms: Difficulty remembering names and recent events is often an early clinical symptom; apathy and depression are also often early symptoms. Later symptoms include impaired judgment, disorientation, confusion, behavior changes and difficulty speaking, swallowing and walking. Revised guidelines for diagnosing Alzheimer's were published in 2011 recommending that Alzheimer's be considered a slowly progressive brain disease that begins well before symptoms emerge.

Brain changes: Hallmark abnormalities are deposits of the protein fragment beta-amyloid (plaques) and twisted strands of the protein tau (tangles) as well as evidence of nerve cell damage and death in the brain.

VASCULAR DEMENTIA

Previously known as multi-infarct or post-stroke dementia, vascular dementia is the second most common cause of dementia after Alzheimer's disease.

Symptoms: Impaired judgment or ability to plan steps needed to complete a task is more likely to be the initial symptom, as opposed to the memory loss often associated with the initial symptoms of Alzheimer's. Occurs from blood vessel blockage or damage leading to infarcts (strokes) or bleeding in the brain. The location of the brain injury determines how the individual's thinking and physical functioning are affected.

Brain changes: Brain imaging can often detect blood vessel problems implicated in vascular dementia. In the past, evidence for vascular dementia was used to exclude a diagnosis of Alzheimer's disease (and vice versa). That practice is no longer considered consistent with pathologic evidence, which shows that the brain changes of several types of dementia can be present simultaneously. When any two or more types of dementia are present at the same time, the individual is considered to have mixed dementia.

DEMENTIA WITH LEWY BODIES (DLB)

Symptoms: People with dementia with Lewy bodies often have memory loss and thinking problems common in Alzheimer's but are more likely than people with Alzheimer's to have initial or early symptoms such as sleep disturbances, well-formed visual hallucinations, and slowness, gait imbalance or other parkinsonian movement features.

Brain changes: Lewy bodies are abnormal aggregations (or clumps) of the protein alpha-synuclein. When they develop in a part of the brain called the cortex, dementia can result. Alpha-synuclein also aggregates in the brains of people with Parkinson's disease, but the aggregates may appear in a pattern that is different from dementia with Lewy bodies.

The brain changes of dementia with Lewy bodies alone can cause dementia, or they can be present at the same time as the brain changes of Alzheimer's disease and/or vascular dementia, with each abnormality contributing to the development of dementia. When this happens, the individual is said to have mixed dementia.

MIXED DEMENTIA

In mixed dementia abnormalities linked to more than one cause of dementia occur simultaneously in the brain. Recent studies suggest that mixed dementia is more common than previously thought.

Brain changes: Characterized by the hallmark abnormalities of more than one cause of dementia - most commonly, Alzheimer's and vascular dementia, but also other types, such as dementia with Lewy bodies.

PARKINSON'S DISEASE

As Parkinson's disease progresses, it often results in a progressive dementia similar to dementia with Lewy bodies or Alzheimer's.

Symptoms: Problems with movement are common symptoms of the disease. If dementia develops, symptoms are often similar to dementia with Lewy bodies.

Brain changes: Alpha-synuclein clumps are likely to begin in an area deep in the brain called the substantia nigra. These clumps are thought to cause degeneration of the nerve cells that produce dopamine.

FRONTOTEMPORAL DEMENTIA (PICK'S DISEASE)

Frontotemporal dementia includes dementias such as behavioral variant FTD, primary progressive aphasia, Pick's disease, corticobasal degeneration and progressive supranuclear palsy.

Symptoms: Typical symptoms include changes in personality and behavior and difficulty with language. Nerve cells in the front and side regions of the brain are especially affected.

Brain changes: No distinguishing microscopic abnormality is linked to all cases. People with FTD generally develop symptoms at a younger age (at about age 60) and survive for fewer years than those with Alzheimer's.

CREUTZFELDT-JAKOB DISEASE (MAD COW DISEASE)

CJD is the most common human form of a group of rare, fatal brain disorders affecting people and certain other mammals. Variant CJD ("mad cow disease") occurs in cattle and has been transmitted to people under certain circumstances.

Symptoms: Rapidly fatal disorder that impairs memory and coordination and causes behavior changes.

Brain changes: Results from misfolded prion protein that causes a "domino effect" in which prion protein throughout the brain misfolds and thus malfunctions.

NORMAL PRESSURE HYDROCEPHALUS

Symptoms: Symptoms include difficulty walking, memory loss and inability to control urination.

Brain changes: Caused by the buildup of fluid in the brain. Can sometimes be corrected with surgical installation of a shunt in the brain to drain excess fluid.

HUNTINGTON'S DISEASE

Huntington's disease is a progressive brain disorder caused by a single defective gene on chromosome 4.

Symptoms: Include abnormal involuntary movements, a severe decline in thinking and reasoning skills, and irritability, depression and other mood changes.

Brain changes: The gene defect causes abnormalities in a brain protein that, over time, lead to worsening symptoms.

WERNICKE-KORSAKOFF SYNDROME

Korsakoff syndrome is a chronic memory disorder caused by severe deficiency of thiamine (vitamin B-1). The most common cause is alcohol misuse.

Symptoms: Memory problems may be strikingly severe while other thinking and social skills seem relatively unaffected.

Brain changes: Thiamine helps brain cells produce energy from sugar. When thiamine levels fall too low, brain cells cannot generate enough energy to function properly.

References:

https://www.healthline.com/health/types-dementia#mixed-dementia

https://www.alz.org/dementia/types-of-dementia.asp

What Is Sundowner's Syndrome?

People with Alzheimer's may develop agitation and other behavioral problems, which seem to worsen as the day progresses. To help them cope with "sundowning" symptoms, think "calm" and "structured."   By Dennis Thompson Jr.

Sometimes people with Alzheimer's disease become more and more agitated as afternoon dissolves into evening. They pace and wander about, becoming more and more aggravated as the darkness deepens. Confusion, paranoia, and demanding behavior all become increasingly noticeable. Eventually, the person might yell or even lash out physically because of their growing frustration.

This phenomenon has long been called "sundowning" because of its prevalence during evening hours. Doctors now believe, however, that this behavior has little, if anything, to do with the sun going down. "That term has been around since the 1960s and 1970s and is now a little outdated," says Christopher Callahan, MD, a professor at the Indiana University School of Medicine and director of the Indiana University Center for Aging Research in Indianapolis. "The notion used to be that when the sun went down and it got dark outside, there were less external stimuli, and patients would get confused." But doctors now say that symptoms associated with sundowner's syndrome can occur at any point during the day or night in Alzheimer's patients.

Still, an estimated 12 to 25 percent of people with Alzheimer's experience this phenomenon, so if you're caring for a loved one with the disease, it's important to know how to handle sundowning symptoms in the event that they present themselves.

Causes of Agitation

Doctors now believe that agitation can occur in Alzheimer's patients for a number of reasons, many of them overlapping. Underlying factors involved in the development of so-called sundowning symptoms can include:

- **Feeling tired and overwhelmed.** "Your brain is often vulnerable after eight hours of being awake. You're tired and you can't handle stimulation as well, you aren't processing it," says Malaz Boustani, MD, a researcher with the Regenstrief Institute and the Indiana University Center for Aging Research, both in Indianapolis.

- **Having a biological clock that is out of whack.** Suffering a hormone imbalance or reacting to other issues that disturb one's "biological clock" can lead to sundowning symptoms. A common cause of biological clock disturbance, for instance, is a lack of exposure to sunlight.

- **Changing routines.** For those accustomed to daylong activities, a lull in their afternoon or evening schedule can cause them to grow bored and restless.

- **Suffering depression symptoms.** People with Alzheimer's may feel depressed and as a result may have trouble in their daily functioning, increasing their potential for agitation.

Some doctors believe that the caregiver or facility looking after the Alzheimer's patient can also be a reason for the person's behavior. "You see it most of the time in an institutional situation," Dr. Boustani says. If your loved one is cared for in a nursing facility or by other hired help, Dr. Boustani recommends looking at sundowning symptoms as "a red flag that the staffing isn't adequate or skilled enough to meet the needs of Alzheimer's patients."

For example, the caregiver could be inadvertently communicating stress or fatigue to the Alzheimer's patient, making the person nervous or anxious. Or a nursing home may regularly have a sudden increase in stimulation late in the day, through noise or social interactions, which can then make the person with Alzheimer's agitated. Even bright lights kept on all night can lead to irritation in an Alzheimer's patient.

Easing Sundowning Symptoms: Begin with a Structured, Calm Day
The best way to keep people with Alzheimer's from becoming agitated is to introduce some structure and peace into their daily routine. The following tips can help:

- **Maintain a regular schedule.** Wake the person at the same time every day and provide meals on a regular schedule each day. Make bedtime the same time every day, too.

- **Limit caffeine.** Be aware of the caffeine content in any food or drinks that your loved one consumes and limit intake as much as possible, especially in the afternoon and evening.

- **Provide regular activity.** It's important to keep people with Alzheimer's involved or interested in activities during the day; this will not only distract them from the agitation and confusion of Alzheimer's but it also discourages napping so that the person is able to fall asleep at bedtime. Activities that incorporate exercise are encouraged as they burn up additional energy and make it easier for the patient to sleep at night. A daily walk, which benefits both the patient and the caregiver, is often recommended, for instance.

- **Wind down the day.** As it gets closer to the person's bedtime, gradually decreasing the amount of stimulation the person experiences will help them to calm down. Turn down the sound on radios, televisions, and stereos and try to keep the home as dark as possible. Limit evening visitors and move noisy family activities to another part of the house, away from the person with Alzheimer's.

- **Seek out medical help.** If your loved one is unable to become calm enough to get to sleep at night, visit your doctor — he or she can look into other medical conditions that might be making it difficult for your loved one to sleep, and can recommend specific treatments.

STAGES OF ALZHEIMERS

Alzheimer's disease typically progresses slowly in three general stages — mild (early-stage), moderate (middle-stage), and severe (late-stage). Since Alzheimer's affects people in different ways, each person will experience symptoms - or progress through Alzheimer's stages differently.

Overview of disease progression

The symptoms of Alzheimer's disease worsen over time, although the rate at which the disease progresses varies. On average, a person with Alzheimer's lives four to eight years after diagnosis, but can live as long as 20 years, depending on other factors.

Changes in the brain related to Alzheimer's begin years before any signs of the disease. This time period, which can last for years, is referred to as preclinical Alzheimer's disease.

The stages below provide an overall idea of how abilities change once symptoms appear and should only be used as a general guide. They are separated into three different categories: mild Alzheimer's disease, moderate Alzheimer's disease and severe Alzheimer's disease. Be aware that it may be difficult to place a person with Alzheimer's in a specific stage as stages may overlap.

Mild Alzheimer's disease (early-stage)

In the early stage of Alzheimer's, a person may function independently. He or she may still drive, work and be part of social activities. Despite this, the person may feel as if he or she is having memory lapses, such as forgetting familiar words or the location of everyday objects.

Friends, family or others close to the individual begin to notice difficulties. During a detailed medical interview, doctors may be able to detect problems in memory or concentration. Common difficulties include:

- Problems coming up with the right word or name
- Trouble remembering names when introduced to new people
- Challenges performing tasks in social or work settings.
- Forgetting material that one has just read
- Losing or misplacing a valuable object
- Increasing trouble with planning or organizing

Moderate Alzheimer's disease (middle-stage)

Moderate Alzheimer's is typically the longest stage and can last for many years. As the disease progresses, the person with Alzheimer's will require a greater level of care.

You may notice the person with Alzheimer's confusing words, getting frustrated or angry, or acting in unexpected ways, such as refusing to bathe. Damage to nerve cells in the brain can make it difficult to express thoughts and perform routine tasks.

At this point, symptoms will be noticeable to others and may include:

- Forgetfulness of events or about one's own personal history
- Feeling moody or withdrawn, especially in socially or mentally challenging situations
- Being unable to recall their own address or telephone number or the high school or college from which they graduated
- Confusion about where they are or what day it is
- The need for help choosing proper clothing for the season or the occasion
- Trouble controlling bladder and bowels in some individuals
- Changes in sleep patterns, such as sleeping during the day and becoming restless at night
- An increased risk of wandering and becoming lost
- Personality and behavioral changes, including suspiciousness and delusions or compulsive, repetitive behavior like hand-wringing or tissue shredding

Severe Alzheimer's disease (late-stage)

In the final stage of this disease, individuals lose the ability to respond to their environment, to carry on a conversation and, eventually, to control movement. They may still say words or phrases, but communicating pain becomes difficult. As memory and cognitive skills continue to worsen, significant personality changes may take place and individuals need extensive help with daily activities.

At this stage, individuals may:

- Need round-the-clock assistance with daily activities and personal care
- Lose awareness of recent experiences as well as of their surroundings
- Experience changes in physical abilities, including the ability to walk, sit and, eventually, swallow
- Have increasing difficulty communicating

Become vulnerable to infections, especially pneumonia

Chapter 16

DEATH & THE PHYSICAL BODY

This chapter deals with sensitive information about death and the physical body. I placed articles here for reading review and education regarding The Dying Process, End of Life Nutrition and Terminal Restlessness/Agitation. These are areas that family and caregiver(s) are unfamiliar with but need to be spoken so that the expectation of how to handle the situation as it arises, eases the guilt and discomfort of the family/caregiver and offers them peace of mind regarding the process of dying. I hope you find this information helpful and it gives you comfort knowing your loved one is not suffering.

Not all dying symptoms show up in every person, but most people experience some combination of the following:

1. Loss of appetite

Energy needs decline. The person may begin to resist or refuse meals and liquids, or accept only small amounts of bland foods (such as hot cereals). Meat, which is hard to digest, may be refused first. Even favorite foods hold little appeal. Near the very end of life, the dying person may be physically unable to swallow.

> *How to respond:* Don't force-feed; follow the person's cues even though you may be distressed by a loss of interest in eating. Periodically offer ice chips, a popsicle, or sips of water. Use a moistened warm cloth around the mouth and apply balm to the lips to keep them moist and comfortable.

2. Excessive fatigue and sleep

The person may begin to sleep the majority of the day and night as metabolism slows and the decline in food and water contribute to dehydration. He or she becomes difficult to rouse from sleep. The fatigue is so pronounced that awareness of immediate surroundings begins to drift.

How to respond: Permit sleep. Avoid jostling the person awake. Assume that everything you say can be heard, as the sense of hearing is thought to persist, even when the person is unconscious, in a coma, or otherwise not responsive.

3. Increased physical weakness

A decline in food intake and lack of energy leads to less energy, even for activities like lifting one's head or shifting in bed. The person may even have difficulty sipping from a straw.

How to respond: Focus on keeping the person comfortable.

4. Mental confusion or disorientation

Organs begin to fail, including the brain. Higher-order consciousness tends to change. "Few conditions leave people hyperaware when they're dying," says palliative-care physician **Ira Byock**, author of *Dying Well*. The person may not be aware of where he or she is or who else is in the room, may speak or reply less often, may respond to people who can't be seen in the room by others (see Passing Away: What to Expect When Witnessing a Loved One's Death), may seem to say nonsensical things, may be confused about time, or may act restless and pick at bed linens.

How to respond: Remain calm and reassuring. Speak to the person softly, and identify yourself when you approach.

5. Labored breathing

Breath intakes and exhales become raggedy, irregular, and labored. A distinctive pattern called Cheyne-Stokes respiration might be heard: a loud, deep inhalation is followed by a pause of not breathing (apnea) for between five seconds to as long as a full minute, before a loud, deep breath resumes and again slowly peters out. Sometimes excessive secretions create loud, gurgling inhalations and exhalations that some people call a "death rattle."

How to respond: The stopped breathing or loud rattle can be alarming to listeners, but the dying person is unaware of this changed breathing; focus on overall comfort. Positions that may help: the head slightly elevated with a pillow, sitting up well-supported, or the head or lying body tilted to the side slightly. Moisten the mouth with a wet cloth and moisturize with lip balm or petroleum jelly. If there's a lot of phlegm, allow it to drain naturally from the mouth, since suctioning it out can increase its quantity. A vaporizer in the room might help. Some people are given oxygen for comfort. Be a calm, physical presence, stroking the arm or speaking softly.

6. Social withdrawal

As the body shuts down, the dying person may gradually lose interest in those nearby. He or she may stop talking or mutter unintelligibly, stop responding to questions, or simply turn away. A few days before receding socially for the last time, the dying person sometimes surprises loved ones with an unexpected burst of alert, attentive behavior. This can last less than an hour or up to a full day.

How to respond: Be aware that this is a natural part of the dying process and not a reflection of your relationship. Maintain a physical presence by touching the dying person and continuing to talk, if it feels appropriate, without demanding anything back. Treasure an alert interlude if and when it occurs, because it's almost always fleeting.

7. Changes in urination

Little going in (as the person loses interest in food and drink) means little coming out. Dropping blood pressure, part of the dying process (and therefore not treated at this point, in tandem with other symptoms), also contributes to the kidneys shutting down. The concentrated urine is brownish, reddish, or tea-colored. Loss of bladder and bowel control may happen late in the dying process.

How to respond: Hospice medical staff sometimes decides that a catheter is necessary, although not in the final hours of life. Kidney failure can increase blood toxins and contribute to a peaceful coma before death. Add a bed pad when placing fresh sheets.

8. Swelling in the feet and ankles

As the kidneys are less able to process bodily fluids, they can accumulate and get deposited in areas of the body away from the heart, in the feet and ankles especially. These places, and sometimes also the hands, face, or feet, take on a swollen, puffy appearance.

> *How to respond:* Usually no special treatment (such as diuretics) is given when the swelling seems directly related to the dying process. (The swelling is the result of the natural death process, not its cause.)

9. Coolness in the tips of the fingers and toes

In the hours or minutes before death, blood circulation draws back from the periphery of the body to help the vital organs. As this happens, the extremities (hands, feet, fingers, toes) become notably cooler. Nail beds may also look more pale, or bluish.

> *How to respond:* A warm blanket can keep the person comfortable, or he or she may be oblivious. The person may complain about the weight of coverings on the legs, so keep them loose.

10. Mottled veins

Skin that had been uniformly pale or ashen develops a distinctive pattern of purplish/reddish/bluish mottling as one of the later signs of death approaching. This is the result of reduced blood circulation. It may be seen first on the soles of the feet.

> *How to respond:* No special steps need to be taken.

** *Note:* These general signs of impending death can vary in sequence and combination from person to person. If a person is on life support (respirator, feeding tube), the process of dying can be different. The signs of death listed here describe a natural dying process.

Chapter 17
THE DYING PROCESS

THE TIMEFRAME:

Months Prior to Death – 1 to 3 months

Withdrawal

As the knowledge that "yes, I'm dying" becomes real, a person begins to withdraw from the world around them. This is the beginning of separation, first from the world-no more interest in newspapers or television, then from people-no more neighbors visiting. This is beginning a time of withdrawing from everything outside of one's self and going inside where
There is sorting out, processing of one's self and one's life.

During this internal processing it is usually done with the eyes closed, so sleep increases. Staying in bed all day and spending more time asleep
becomes the norm. With this withdrawal comes less of a need to communicate with others. Words are seen as being connected with the physical life that is being left behind. Words and speaking become less important and touch becomes more meaningful.

Food

Food is the way we energize our body. It is the means by which we keep our body alive. It is natural that when a body is preparing to die, it will require less food. There is a gradual decrease in appetite. When the person wants little or no fluid or food, this indicates that your loved one's body is preparing to shut down. Do not try to force food or liquid into the person, or try to use guilt or manipulate them into eating or drinking something. To do this only makes the person more uncomfortable.

- Do offer small chips of ice, frozen Gatorade, popsicles or juice which may be refreshing in the mouth' If the person can swallow.
- Don't force fluids or food. It is perfectly normal and alright not to eat.

Pain and fear are reactions to approaching death and may cause you to feel that the pain is not being adequately controlled. Be assured that not all restlessness are indications of pain and the discomfort. Remember that anxiety about pain often increases pain.

Permission

Giving permission to your loved one to let go without feeling guilty for leaving or trying to keep him/her with you to meet your own needs can be difficult.

A dying person will try to hold on, though it brings prolonged discomfort, in order to be sure that those left behind will be alright. Therefore, ability to release the dying person from this concern and give assurance that it is alright to let go whenever they are ready, is one of the greatest gifts you can give your loved one at this time.

Pain

There is a difference between pain and suffering. There are also different kinds of pain:
- Physical
- social (withdrawal from family and loved ones)
- psychological
- spiritual (feeling estranged from God)

During this time attention must be paid to the psycho-social aspects of pain; they are suffering and the impact on physical pain.

Pain stems from an organic cause and each person responds to pain in an individual way. People who ask for medications when they are dying are not drug addicts.

What happens to the physical body when we are dying? The answers are in the next few pages can assist in understanding the process of our bodies in our last days or hours.

ACTIVE DYING STAGES

Signs of the Preactive Phase of Dying:

- increased restlessness, confusion, agitation, inability to stay content in one position and insisting on changing positions frequently (exhausting family and caregivers)
- withdrawal from active participation in social activities
- increased periods of sleep, lethargy
- decreased intake of food and liquids
- beginning to show periods of pausing in the breathing (apnea) whether awake or sleeping
- patient reports seeing persons who had already died
- patient states that he or she is dying
- patient requests family visit to settle "unfinished business" and tie up "loose ends"inability to heal or recover from wounds or infections increased swelling (edema) of either the extremities or the entire body

Signs of the Active Phase of Dying

- inability to arouse patient at all (coma) or, ability to only arouse patient with great effort but patient quickly returns to severely unresponsive state (semi-coma)
- severe agitation in patient, hallucinations, acting "crazy" and not in patient's normal manner or personality
- much longer periods of pausing in the breathing (apnea)
- dramatic changes in the breathing pattern including apnea, but also including very rapid breathing or cyclic changes in the patterns of breathing (such as slow progressing to very fast and then slow again, or shallow progressing to very deep breathing while also changing rate of breathing to very fast and then slow)
- other very abnormal breathing patterns

- severely increased respiratory congestion or fluid buildup in lungs
- inability to swallow any fluids at all (not taking any food by mouth voluntarily as well)
- patient states that he or she is going to die
- patient breathing through wide open mouth continuously and no longer can speak even if awake
- urinary or bowel incontinence in a patient who was not incontinent before
- marked decrease in urine output and darkening color of urine or very abnormal colors (such as red or brown)
- blood pressure dropping dramatically *from patient's normal* blood pressure range (more than a 20 or 30-point drop)
- systolic blood pressure below 70, diastolic blood pressure below 50
- patient's extremities (such as hands, arms, feet and legs) feel very cold to touch
- patient complains that his or her legs/feet are numb and cannot be felt at all
- cyanosis, or a bluish or purple coloring to the patients arms and legs, especially the feet and hands)
- patient's body is held in rigid unchanging position
- jaw drop; the patient's jaw is no longer held straight and may drop to the side their head is lying towards

Although all patients do not show all of these signs, many of these signs will be seen in some patients. The reason for the tradition of "keeping a vigil" when someone is dying is that we really don't know exactly when death will occur until it is obviously happening.

Chapter 18
END OF LIFE NUTRITION

In the final days and weeks of life, many patients reduce food and fluid intake, resulting in weight loss or cachexia. These physical changes may upset and puzzle family members, who misperceive end-of-life anorexia as the cause of death rather than as part of the dying process. Some patients and family members, in consultation with those healthcare professionals who believe that ensuring proper intake of nutrients and fluids is essential at all stages of life (even at the expense of comfort and quality of life), may consider percutaneous endoscopic gastrostomy (PEG) tube feeding. The evidence suggests administering nutrients neither prolongs nor improves life for many elderly patients with anorexia-related malnutrition at the end of life, and weight loss and cachexia frequently persist despite intervention. Thus, many registered dietitians consider the phrase end-of-life nutrition care an oxymoron.

All healthcare professionals in long-term care should understand the current evidence-based recommendations for end-of-life nutrition care. It is imperative that they provide patients, families, and surrogates with accurate information regarding the risks and benefits of PEG tube feeding and other means of artificial nutrition and hydration (ANH) for patients approaching the end of life.

Foregoing Artificial Nutrition and Hydration at the End of Life

The evidence suggests that withholding Artificial Nutrition & Hydration (ANH) is neither painful nor uncomfortable. People adapt physiologically to starvation, and studies show that dying patients who stop eating and drinking rarely experience discomfort due to hunger. Dehydration usually precedes starvation, causing hemoconcentration (increase in the proportion of formed elements in the blood, as a result of a decrease in its fluid content) and hyperosmolality (draw water from cells by osmosis). This is followed by azotemia (relating to filtering of the kidneys), hypernatremia (decrease of water in the body), and hypercalcemia (elevated levels of calcium)

**These metabolic changes are thought to have a sedating effect on the brain prior to death, and some think dehydration may increase comfort and minimize pain during the dying process.

Withholding or minimizing hydration in the final days of life can also have desirable effects, including a reduction in oral and bronchial secretions, a decreased need to urinate, and less pulmonary congestion and associated coughing.

Ice chips, moistened swabs, and proper mouth care can help manage dry mouth in dehydrated patients. Patients who are no longer eating or drinking may exhibit confusion, delirium, and diminished alertness, but these effects are typically associated with the active dying process and can occur with any progressive illness regardless of food and fluid consumption.

Keep in mind that even when a healthy person gets sick they lose their appetite. This is because your body is focusing the energy on healing your body instead of digesting your food. Digestion takes a lot of the body's energy source which also explains why you want to take a nap after a meal.

The following is an interesting article you can look up via the link below regarding fasting and how it affects the brain in a positive physical and spiritual way.

http://humansarefree.com/2013/12/fasting-supercharges-your-brain-here-is.html

A Regulatory Perspective - for Clinicians

Out of necessity, practitioners in the skilled nursing environment are concerned with how the Centers for Medicare & Medicaid Services (CMS) will view end-of-life nutrition plans for residents. According to CMS's State Operations Manual, all care and services provided for nutrition and hydration, including comfort measures, should be based on the resident's choices and the results of a pertinent nutritional assessment. CMS acknowledges that when end-of-life care is provided according to an individualized care plan that gives priority to the resident's choices, residents with terminal conditions may fail to meet acceptable parameters of nutritional status. As long as a facility has documentation that the plan of care was discussed with the resident or his or her family or surrogate and that it complies with their wishes, CMS is not likely to question the use of hand feeding rather than tube feeding for a terminally ill resident.

In Conclusion

Healthcare professionals, patients, and families should recognize that tube placement is not a risk-free medical intervention and understand the burdens it may impose on the patient. The risks and benefits of PEG tube insertion for terminally ill patients should be carefully assessed and discussed between the IDT, the patient, and the patient's family or surrogate to help ensure that all decisions about end-of-life nutrition are informed and appropriate.

Resource: www.annalsoflongtermcare.com/content/nutrition-end-life-tube-feeding-solution#sthash.7YSud8RH.dpuf

Chapter 19

TERMINAL AGITATION or RESTLESSNESS

Many families may be surprised when a terminally ill (and usually calm) family member becomes restless or even agitated. The depth of such restlessness or agitation varies from patient to patient. When moods change or personalities seem to change, family members may be completely bewildered and feel helpless: not knowing what to do. It is common knowledge that individuals who are experiencing even minor illnesses may demonstrate mood changes such as irritability, anger, depression and avoid communication with others. When a terminal illness not only initially strikes, but is now nearing the end, patients may experience profound mood changes. Such mood changes are often difficult for family members to "handle." Causes and treatments for restlessness and agitation are well-known among the palliative care professionals who work with the dying on a regular basis.

What is Terminal Restlessness or Agitation?

Those who work with the dying know this type of restlessness or agitation almost immediately. However, the public and patient's family may have no idea what is going on and often become quite alarmed at their loved one's condition. What does it look like? Although it varies somewhat in each patient, there are common themes that are seen over and over again.

Patients may be too weak to walk or stand, but they insist on getting up from the bed to the chair, or from the chair back to the bed. Whatever position they are in, they complain they are not comfortable and demand to change positions, even if pain is well managed. They may yell out using uncharacteristic language, sometimes angrily accusing others around them.

They appear extremely agitated and may not be objective about their own condition. They may be hallucinating, having psychotic episodes and be totally "out of control." At these times, the patient's safety is seriously threatened.

Some patients may demand to go to the hospital emergency room, even though there is nothing that can be done for them there. Some patients may insist that the police be called ... that someone unseen is trying to harm them. Some patients may not recognize those around them, confusing them with other people. They may act as if they were living in the past, confronting an old enemy.

While I have educated many over the years about Terminal Agitation, I had never actually witnessed it for myself. That is until my brother suffered from it off and on during his last three months of life. In the final days he had a severe case of agitation that was completely opposite his personality. I learned firsthand how devastating it is to see this symptom in your dying loved one.

Fortunately, it only lasted 32 hours and then he progressed on to a more peaceful state of mind and body. Again, giving thanks to those in the hospice field that were there to assist him and our family during this most difficult process.

Resource: http://www.hospicepatients.org/terminal-agitation.html

Terminal Agitation

Terminal agitation often surprises many family members and caregivers alike. The loved one who is usually calm, suddenly and unexpectedly becomes agitated and restless. As patients near the end of a terminal illness they may experience profound mood changes. Therefore, terminal agitation is often accompanied by mood swings or personality changes which leave caregivers feeling helpless and bewildered. The sudden onset of behavior changes differentiates terminal agitation from the personality changes of dementia which are usually gradual.

Related Behaviors

BEHAVIORS

Agitation
Extreme emotional disturbance; perturbation
- Anger
- Despair
- Combativeness
- Irritability
- Striking out
- Grimacing

Anxiety
State of uneasiness and apprehension
- Nervousness
- Tearfulness
- Tension
- Fear
- Anguish
- Furrowed brow
- No eye contact
- Wild-eyed look

Distress
Anxiety or mental suffering
Behaviors listed under both agitation and anxiety included here

RESTLESSNESS
Not able to rest, relax or be still

- Repetitive movement
- Constant moving or motion
- Inability to be still
- Movement
- Unable to rest
- Constantly changing positions
- Movement of limbs
- Increased movement
- Non-purposeful motor activity
- Hyperactivity
- Tossing and turning
- Busyness
- Thrashing/flailing
- Can not get comfortable
- Head rolling
- Trying to get out of bed
- Fidgeting/squirming
- Unsettled
- Shifting from side to side
- Jerking
- Pulling/picking at clothes and sheets
- Removing clothes and sheets
- Climbing out of bed
- Grabbing people
- Rocking

SLEEP ISSUES

- Inability to sleep
- Wakefulness/insomnia
- Impaired sleep
- Sleep disturbance

VERBALIZATIONS

- Singing/humming
- Confused speech
- Incoherent speech patterns
- Unintelligible babble
- Calling out
- Moaning/groaning
- Crying
- Rhythmic vocalizations

MENTAL STATE

- Hallucinations
- Altered level of consciousness
- Confusion
- Incoherence
- Paranoia
- Disorientation
- Inability to concentrate
- Difficulty focusing

Management

Treat any underlying issues, such as:
- Pain
- Full bladder
- Spiritual distress
- Emotional distress

Patient/Caregiver Support
- Create a calm and safe environment
- Attempt to re-orient the patient as possible
- Educate the family on what is occurring as this can be a fearful time
- Encourage family assistance, as appropriate

Medications
- Ativan
- Haldol
- Thorazine
- Versed

Statistics

According to the National Hospice and Palliative Care Organization and Hospice Pharmacia, 42% of dying patients experience terminal restlessness in the final 48 hours of life.

The agitation is a terminal event, occurring only in the very last hours of life. It is NOT to be confused with the anguish and distress of many patients who are not yet dying and who need company and counseling and NOT sedatives.

It is important to eliminate other causes

- ❏ Does the patient have an infection?
- ❏ Is pain under control?
- ❏ Is the patient having any psychosocial or emotional issues?
- ❏ When was the last bowel movement?
- ❏ Does the patient have a fever?
- ❏ Does the patient have any breathing difficulty?
- ❏ Is the patient's bladder full?
- ❏ Has the patient received any new medication?
- ❏ Is anything physically interfering with the patient's comfort (ex: wrinkled sheets, room temperature)?

** Please contact author for a full-page copy of this document

Chapter 20

RESOURCES & NETWORKS

Throughout this book there are several resource links and more below as helpful resources and I encourage you to review each one and contact them for assistance with your unique situation.

Area Agency on Aging
http://www.n4a.org/

Elder Care Directory - federal
http://www.eldercaredirectory.org/federal.htm

Assistance with bill pay for seniors – federal
http://www.eldercaredirectory.org/federal.htm

Aging Care
www.agingcare.com

Caregiver resources:

Caring From a Distance (www.cfad.org; 202-895-9465)

Family Caregiver Alliance (www.caregiver.org; 800-445-8106)

National Family Caregivers Association (www.nfcacares.org; 800-896-3650)

National Respite Network (www.archrespite.org; 703-256-2084)

AARP (www.aarp.org/families/caregiving; 888-687-2277)

https://www.medicare.gov/campaigns/caregiver/caregiver-resource-kit.html

http://www.caregiving.org/resources/

Advance Directives Information:
http://familydoctor.org/familydoctor/en/healthcare-management/end-of-life-issues/advance-directives-and-do-not-resuscitate-orders.html

http://liv-will1.uslivingwillregistry.com/individuals.html

Some final thoughts, Author Unknown:

I reached the pinnacle of success in the business world. In others' eyes, my life is an epitome of success. However, aside from work, I have little joy. In the end, wealth is only a fact of life that I am accustomed to.

At this moment, lying on the sick bed and recalling my whole life, I realize that all the recognition and wealth that I took so much pride in, have paled and become meaningless in the face of impending death. In the darkness, I look at the green lights from the life supporting machines and hear the humming mechanical sounds; I can feel the breath of god of death drawing closer...

Now I know, when we have accumulated sufficient wealth to last our lifetime, we should pursue other matters that are unrelated to wealth...
Should be something that is more important, perhaps relationships, perhaps art, perhaps a dream from younger days ...

Non-stop pursuing of wealth will only turn a person into a twisted being, just like me. God gave us the senses to let us feel the love in everyone's heart, not the illusions brought about by wealth. The wealth I have won in my life I cannot bring with me. What I can bring is only the memories precipitated by love. That's the true riches which will follow you, accompany you, giving you strength and light to go on.

Love can travel a thousand miles. Life has no limit. Go where you want to go. Reach the height you want to reach. It is all in your heart and in your hands.

What is the most expensive bed in the world? - "Sick bed" ...

You can employ someone to drive the car for you, make money for you but you cannot have someone to bear the sickness for you.

Material things lost can be found. But there is one thing that can never be found when it is lost – "Life".

When a person goes into the operating room, he will realize that there is one book that he has yet to finish reading – "Book of Healthy Life". Whichever stage in life we are at right now, with time, we will face the day when the curtain comes down.

Treasure Love for your family, love for your spouse, love for your friends...
Treat yourself well. Cherish others.

(It was thought this was from Steve Jobs in his last days but there is no definitive evidence of such. It is, however, very profound)

ABOUT THE AUTHOR

Barbara has worked in the field of hospice for several years as an educator and liaison. Many times, she has been the first person to have the discussion about the reality regarding end of life for the family and their loved one. She herself has lost her immediate family over the years and explains that while she has been surrounded by death during her lifetime, she lives life to the fullest and believes in giving rather than receiving.

"For it is in the giving that we truly lose ourselves only to find the real meaning in life... love."

My personal experience is one of grief and loss throughout my lifetime staring when I was 15 years old with the loss of my middle brother Anthony, who was killed by a drunk driver. In later years, I lost my father to COPD and Pancreatic Cancer. Shortly afterwards, my I lost my mother who gently passed away in her sleep. Most recently my oldest sibling and brother Robert lost his battle to lung cancer on his birthday, to which this book is dedicated.

I understand the immense feelings and emotions that are involved with the loss of a loved one and receiving that diagnosis of finality. I have a unique perspective of terminal illness as well because I am a cancer survivor. Diagnosed in 2007 with ovarian cancer, I feel that God has a plan and his will be done. It is a blessing to serve others on the last leg of their journey offering peace and reassurance for their Celestial discharge. If could offer one small piece of guidance, I would simply say to live in the present and forget the past...just love in the moment. Embrace those around you and know that it can all change and be gone in the blink of an eye, so seize the day and make your life count!

"A Touching Testimonial"

Sent: Thursday, July 11, 2013 04:31 PM
To: Barbara Ball
Subject: You are an angel!

Dear Barbara,

I am sorry that this can't be a longer, more formal letter, but our lives are chaotic right now, as you will understand. I am writing to express our family's gratitude to you and your organization for acting so quickly, and in such a Herculean way. You moved our dad to your hospice facility in just a matter of hours and the day before a holiday. Very impressive!

You really showed the spirit of compassion in all of your dealings with dad and with us, his family, for those several hours that we were together. You were focused on our immediate needs and worked diligently and creatively to get to a quick resolution that evening.

I was sorry that dad didn't live long enough to enjoy your facility, but you definitely made a difference in his last few days. He was grateful for all of your effort, and that of the others involved that afternoon, to find a suitable place for him. We are comforted by the fact that he didn't die alone, at home, in his chair, unable to move or even call for help. This was a much better end - cleaned, fed, cared for, respected and treated humanely.

We can't thank you enough! You were an angel sent to us that day. God bless you!

Dave – Son of hospice patient

IN CONCLUSION:

I hope that this little book has given some clarity regarding what healthcare services are about and offered some direction for you and your family.

As a healthcare worker in the field of hospice for many years, I found these questions were unanswered or unknown to inquire about. My hope is to assist you with making a better and more informed decision regarding your aging parent or loved one.

Advocating for the Public and the Elderly

Legacy Advocates
legacyadaz@gmail.com

My wish for you is peace and love in your journey here on this Earth and comfort for you and your loved ones.

Barbara Ball

REFERENCES

Ellen Kubler-Ross – The 5 Stages of Grief

http://grief.com/the-five-stages-of-grief/

https://en.wikipedia.org/wiki/K%C3%BCbler-Ross_model

http://changingminds.org/disciplines/change_management/kubler_ross/kubler_ross.htm

http://www.cremationresource.org/cremation/how-to-decide-whether-to-cremate-or-bury.html

And included on each page with reference materials quoted

This book can be purchased direct through the author at:

https://www.createspace.com/5990817

Directly Available on Amazon

"Life is not measured by how many breaths we take, but by how many moments take our breath away"

My family - The Earl O. Ball Family